✦ *Profession of English*

✦ *Other books by G. B. Harrison*

Author

THE ELIZABETHAN AND JACOBEAN JOURNALS: BEING A RECORD OF THOSE THINGS MOST TALKED OF DURING THE YEARS 1591-1610 (5 VOLS.)

SHAKESPEARE AT WORK 1591-1603

ELIZABETHAN PLAYS AND PLAYERS

THE LIFE AND DEATH OF ROBERT DEVEREUX, EARL OF ESSEX

SHAKESPEARE'S TRAGEDIES

INTRODUCING SHAKESPEARE

JOHN BUNYAN: A STUDY IN PERSONALITY

THE FIRES OF ARCADIA

Editor

THE BODLEY HEAD QUARTOS

THE CHURCH BOOK OF BUNYAN MEETING

NICHOLAS BRETON'S MELANCHOLIKE HUMOURS

THE TRIAL OF THE LANCASTER WITCHES, 1612

DE MAISSE'S JOURNAL (EDITED AND TRANSLATED, WITH R. A. JONES)

SHAKESPEARE: THE COMPLETE WORKS

General Editor

THE SHAKESPEARE ASSOCIATION FACSIMILES

MAJOR BRITISH WRITERS

A COMPANION TO SHAKESPEARE STUDIES (WITH HARLEY GRANVILLE-BARKER)

PROFESSION OF ENGLISH

G. B. HARRISON

A HARVEST BOOK

HARCOURT BRACE JOVANOVICH, INC., NEW YORK

ACKNOWLEDGMENT

I wish to thank those colleagues who read portions of this book in typescript, and to exonerate them from any responsibility for the final version. I would also thank Mr. Gilbert Highet and Alfred A. Knopf, Inc. for permission to use the passage from *The Art of Teaching* quoted on pages 172-173.

Printed in the United States of America

A B C D E F G H I J

Library of Congress Cataloging in Publication Data

Harrison, George Bagshawe, date
Profession of English.

(A Harvest book, HB 257)
1. English literature—Study and teaching (Higher). 2. Education, Higher. I. Title.
[PR35.H3 1973] 820'.7 73-5607
ISBN 0-15-674650-6 (pbk.)

To W. G. R.

NOTE TO THE HARVEST EDITION

Since this book was first written, the organization and conditions of English education have changed in many ways. The account of the public schools and universities given on pages 31 through 49 should therefore be regarded as historical rather than contemporary.

G. B. H., 1973

✦ Contents

✦ *Profession of English*

PROLOGUE ✦ *The Questions*

My graduate assistant and I were standing in the corridor outside 2231 Angell Hall at the University of Michigan, waiting for the lecture to begin. Suddenly he remarked, "I wish you would tell me what you are trying to accomplish in your teaching and study of English literature. And why?"

It might seem obvious that any person who teaches English in a university should have a ready and immediate answer which he would long ago have passed on to his students. In fact, it is not so. Once, at a time when the syllabus for the Honors Degree in English was being acrimoniously debated at the University of London, I also put these same questions to some of my colleagues. They shied away from me as if I had uttered unclean words. Three of the embarrassed replies I recorded.

One was from a distinguished Head of a Department, much

esteemed by his colleagues and by himself. He answered severely: "I am sure we are all agreed on the purposes of our Honors degrees in English."

The second, also Head of a Department, and later Professor Emeritus, replied, "I don't believe much in this teaching English literature at all. A butcher is just as capable as I am of passing judgment on literature"—which in his case was certainly true.

A third—a woman lecturer in Old English—exclaimed: "To produce scholars! To produce scholars like R. W. Chambers!" That was indeed a worthy aim, but so far the late Professor R. W. Chambers has remained unimitated and inimitable.

My questioner and I debated the matter over luncheon. The natural academic reaction to such an inquiry is to fly to authority and to recommend a short course of reading. Indeed, there are several excellent works, which should be chewed and digested, read wholly and with diligence and attention, by anyone who professes to teach the humanities, such as Jacques Barzun's *Teacher in America,* and Gilbert Highet's *The Art of Teaching,* and Bruce Truscot's *Red Brick University*.

But my graduate assistant was insistent. "I don't want books," said he; "I want to know what you yourself believe"—a fair demand, though brutal.

A few days later I spoke of this discussion to one of my mentors at Harcourt, Brace, who happened to be visiting the campus, and I was thereupon peremptorily challenged to give my answers in print, not in the form of a treatise on the teaching of English, but rather as a personal record of my own prejudices and observations after nearly forty years' experience as student, professor and author.

Thus dared, I began to meditate after the pattern laid down by St. Ignatius, which concluded, as all such meditations should, in a *resolution:* I would accept the challenge, and, regardless of the great and obvious risks, set down my own answers to the original questions. *Profession of English* is that record. If the advanced critic finds the book full of antiquated naïveté and perversity, it may best serve him as a kind of there-but-for-the-Grace-of-God; it may even remind him that there are other ways and approaches to the study of literature than his own.

When at length I had finished the record, I thought it might be illuminating to see how some of my friends in the Department of English at the University of Michigan would respond to the challenge. I asked them the same questions, but in writing. Their replies—carefully considered, guarded and therefore elevated—were these: "I study and teach literature because the mastery of its language differentiates the human from the brute, because its aesthetic and historical problems challenge my scholarship, because it helps me, with religion, to discover the coherence of life. . . ."

"In studying and teaching English literature, I aim, generally, to honor and understand the human spirit in its history as that history is written by the poets—that is, by men possessing a comprehensive soul and a genius for language; more specifically, to uphold and even extend the love of good writing and good reading; more broadly again, to show and affirm that out of the mingling and conflicting realms of nature and of ideas is made the human condition proper in which we seek to hold 'eternity in an hour.' . . ."

"For me, literature provides order and meaning to life; I want my students to observe that order (an intellectual exercise) and to comprehend its beauty (an aesthetic experience). . . ."

"All my life I have been enjoying teaching and writing, and I can't give you an answer. So long as men can be found who enjoy teaching the humanities and love the humanities, I have no alarm about the humanities. . . ."

From these replies I concluded that none of them had ever before seriously considered the questions.

Early in the conversation with my original questioner, it became clear that there could be no final, objective or statistical answer to his demands, for the purpose and the meaning of literature grow and change as the experience of reading and study become fuller and deeper. Moreover, the upbringing of my graduate assistant had been so different from mine that the very terms of his questions—"literature," "English" and "study"—meant something different to each of us.

We must begin by brooding over the meaning of our terms.

1 ✦ *Definitions*

I. LITERATURE

Definition is the business of the dictionary makers; but they are not too helpful. For *literature,* the Great Lexicographer is content with "learning; skill in letters." *The Shorter Oxford English Dictionary* is more expansive, from "literary culture (now rare and obsolete)" to "any printed matter." But no professor of literature, not even George Saintsbury, could claim acquaintance with "any printed matter." We must look elsewhere. Since my graduate assistant had been conditioned by his professors of criticism, perhaps I should find my definition in some collection of their pronouncements, such as "*Critiques and Essays in Criticism 1920-1948 Representing the Achievement of Modern British and American Critics,* selected by Robert Wooster Stallman, University of Connecticut; with a foreword by Cleanth Brooks."

This important volume gathers pronouncements of the

most notable critics of this age, which, concludes the editor, "is an age of criticism. The structure of critical ideas and the practical criticism that British critics—Leavis, Turnell, Empson, Read—and American critics—Ransom, Tate, Brooks, Warren, Blackmur, Winters,—have contrived upon the foundations of Eliot and Richards constitute an achievement in literary criticism which has not been equalled in any previous period of our literary history." Here, then, should be found the authentic words of the High Priests, who, however, like other hierophants, alternately flatter and backbite each other.

"Both Tate and Leavis," says Stallman, "derive their critical position from Eliot. They have crystalized and expanded germinal ideas planted in *The Sacred Wood.* As Leavis makes clear in *Education and the University* (1943), he opposes, however, Eliot's doctrinal approach. Both critics reject Richards' theory of art and for the past two decades, they have vigorously assaulted his pseudo-scientific, pseudo-psychological, and semasiological approach."

The editor's triumphant conclusion that this is the great age of critical achievement is hardly in tune with his previous lament, a few pages earlier, that "intellectual chaos has been the background of American poetry and criticism during this period"; its cause, or one of them, "is *the loss of tradition.* We lack a religious and social tradition which would extend moral and intellectual authority to the poet. . . . Never were poets more profoundly divided from the life of society than in our time. . . . The effect is twofold: (1) confusion as to the boundaries of criticism, and (2) extreme individualism in viewpoints —the expression of a personal view of life, the exploitation of personality."

I was disappointed in the High Priests. So I turned to René Wellek and Austin Warren's *Theory of Literature.* They perhaps would guide me out of the Dark Wood. It was not so. They merely multiplied the confusing perplexity of the paths as they enumerated and rejected the different methods and approaches.

While I was thus befogged, there came to me, as once to Philip Sidney, the inner voice. "Fool," said my Muse to me, "look in thy heart and write; and," she added tartly, "don't use any of that polysyllabic technical jargon."

This was hard advice, for our whole academic tradition is against personal statements which cannot be supported by well-established and acknowledged external authority. Yet it is debatable whether this attitude is truly scientific and scholarly, or merely timid reluctance to trust to one's own intuition and experience.

"Muse," I replied diffidently, "you counsel well; but I trust that your advice to be bold and resolute is no witch's riddle to lure me to destruction. If you should deal double with me, truly it were an ill thing to be offered to any academic, and very weak dealing." Could I then propound any definition better than the mythical young woman from Girton who defined literature as "works approved by T. S. Eliot and Dr. Leavis"? I would try.

In terms of courses and syllabuses this word *literature,* which we use so freely, means that they are mainly concerned with poems, dramas, novels, short stories, essays and works of criticism. But a course in literature may also include letters, biographies, histories, works of philosophy, theology and psychology. One quality is common to all; they must give delight by their manner of writing.

Literature, at least by derivation, implies also "recorded in writing"; which is ultimately a record of sound, for words are sounds—sound symbols which by common consent carry an agreed meaning. *Homo sapiens* must have started to use sound symbols almost as early as he was created a separate species. Speech may indeed have been a major cause of his development, for no tribe, seemingly, is without some kind of speech, though the preservation of sound symbols in permanent form is quite late in man's history. Its first use was practical. The human memory is short and fallible, and men often lie. Debts can be denied by debtor and exaggerated by creditor. So there were developed means of recording certain sound symbols in durable materials—notches on sticks of wood, marks on clay, stone or parchment or leather. The earliest writings are records of numbers. When Michael Ventris finally cracked the secret of the Minoan B script, he revealed not pre-Homeric versions of the *Iliad* but lists of names, rations, leases, tribute, furniture and the like.

Other kinds of record were soon needed of laws and customs, contracts and agreements, and also of calendars and reckonings of time. The earliest writing is little more than a rough method of recording facts. Ultimately writing was elaborated to record sounds in such a way that they could be reproduced entire. When this stage is reached, "literature" begins. We are so accustomed, without a second thought, to regard literature as something written that we forget that poems, dramas and other kinds of spoken word need neither to be written nor recorded; but without "writing" they are soon distorted or forgotten.

Sounds thus recorded in writing are far removed from the fact, experience, thought or emotion which they symbolize. First, the experience is converted into the complex sound symbols heard by the ear which in turn are transformed into signs perceived by the eye. Readers must reverse the process, turning the signs seen by the eye into sounds heard in the inward ear. Sounds are then translated into that which they symbolize. In so complex a process inevitably much is lost in the act of transference.

After generations of practice educated readers can now effect the transference from writing to speech instantaneously. As a result two kinds of language have evolved: the spoken word and the written word.

At first, and until recently, writing and print (which is but writing reduplicated) recorded speech so that it could be reproduced as sound. At the beginning of the century many elderly people, and not only the undereducated (my Victorian Aunt Sarah was one), even in silent reading would move their lips. Today most of us read so much that we have acquired the habit of assimilating the meaning of a printed page without first turning it into heard sounds. Many have even been taught that this is the correct way of reading. Much modern writing, especially technical, may convey ideas, but is quite intolerable as spoken speech, as we painfully realize when we listen to the reading of a technical or scientific paper. Economists, sociologists, psychologists, educationists are terrible offenders; and some of the newer critics also.

Speech whether it be written or spoken is an imperfect means of communication, as every lover or mystic knows. How can I say in words what the sunset meant to each of us last night?

Words are hardly adequate to express the commonest objects or the simplest ideas. We cannot even discuss the properties of an equilateral triangle without a diagram, that is, bringing in the eye to help out the ear. Hence the craftsman in words, the poet, unable to express his feelings or emotions literally and directly, not only uses words which by comparison or contrast or association or evocation touch on every sense and experience but he arranges them in patterns of sound, rhythmic and musical, because the ear is peculiarly sensitive to rhythm which stirs up all kinds of emotion. It is spellbinding. In a more direct and more primitive form, the rhythms of jazz also are spellbinders.

There exist in all of us areas of *sensitive spots*—memories of sounds, smells, tastes, feelings, of persons and places, of books and pictures, emotions and experiences, everything that makes up the mind of man. Such areas exist in every man. Each individual has a central core which is personal, intimate and unique; an inner circle which he shares with a few others; and large areas which are common to many. Words function when they touch on sensitive spots and cause them to glow; and not only words, but a host of other stimuli—scents, sights, sounds, touches, gestures, colors. But in everyone the areas both sensitive and insensitive are different; no two hearers have exactly the same response.

This disconcerting fact can easily be verified. From time to time I try the experiment with a class. A poem is read aloud, and each hearer is asked to jot down as honestly as he can what happened in his own mind as he listened. One poem chosen was Blake's "Jerusalem," from his *Milton*.

And did those feet in ancient time
Walk upon England's mountains green?
And was the holy Lamb of God
On England's pleasant pastures seen?

And did the Countenance Divine
Shine forth upon our clouded hills?
And was Jerusalem builded here
Among these dark Satanic Mills?

Bring me my bow of burning gold!
Bring me my arrows of desire!
Bring me my spear! O clouds, unfold!
Bring me my chariot of fire!

I will not cease from mental fight,
Nor shall my sword sleep in my hand,
Till we have built Jerusalem
In England's green and pleasant land.

These were some responses:

A. "Song called Jerusalem. Sung it in grade 5. Remember reference to it in a book discussing question whether Christ ever visited England. Significance given to wattle churches in Somerset—vague legends—Christ's uncle traded in tin—green pastures everywhere—did Christ walk here? Whoever saw a sword sleep?—sounds good when given by a male chorus—Jerusalem, who built Jerusalem?—'builded' isn't right—what has this got to do with Milton? I thought that piece was an old folk song—maybe Blake was a plagiarist—very beautiful soft green fields bounded by woods."

B. " 'Of his earth visiting feet, this much has been told'—

'and lo, that traffic of Jacob's ladder, pitched between Heaven and Charing Cross'—I will be with you all days—Little lamb who made thee?—the description of the charioteer in Shelley's *Prometheus*—the black factories of the Industrial age—drawing a black line across blue heaven—the toil of a nation underground dying in pain. The prophet's angry—Old King Cole—the sound of a million swords—'We answer him with a blaze of swords'—the New Jerusalem—no more mills—but a country of small holdings—the return of the innocence of anger and surprise."

c. "The scene is full of contrast. There are green grassy fields and around them are grey woods—mounds with black mills churning, churning on nothing at all. There is no water around. There is a saint walking around in the grass: a halo is around his head. Above a flaming charioteer is spiralling upward. In this chariot is a Greek god firing arrows ahead of him. A tremendous symphony of Debussy is in progress. The sun is shining bright. Great silver globules called ideals are circling in the sunlit air. It is a bright scene. Victory is in sight, Hurray! hurray! hurrah!"

Blake's poem, though simple, is far from direct statement, and widely different responses might be expected. But even straight prose narrative will produce differences as striking. A second experiment was to read aloud the description of the death of Jezebel from II Kings 9, 30-37 (King James version).

And when Jehu was come to Jezreel, Jezebel heard of it; and she painted her face, and tired her head, and looked out at a window. And as Jehu entered in at the gate, she said, Had Zimri peace, who slew his master? And he lifted up his face to the window, and said, Who is on my side? Who? And there looked out to him two or three eunuchs. And he said, Throw her down. So they threw her down: and some of her blood was sprinkled on the wall, and on the horses: and he trode her under foot. And when he was come in, he did eat and drink, and said, Go, see now this cursed woman, and bury her: for she is a king's daughter. And they went to bury her: but they found no more of her than the skull, and the feet, and the palms of her hands. Wherefore they came again, and told him. And he said, This is the word of the LORD, which he spake by his servant Elijah the Tishbite, saying, In the portion of Jezreel shall dogs eat the flesh of Jezebel: And the carcase of Jezebel shall be as dung upon the face of the field in the portion of Jezreel; so that they shall not say, This is Jezebel.

These were some of the responses:

A. "I can see a black haired woman with a sly leer on her face as she combs her hair. She puts powder over the wickedness of age and evil in her face, and slinks over to the window. Then, catastrophe! Blood and fury—she falls to her death. A sort of surrealist painting springs up into view. I see feet broken off from the ankles. I see fingers torn away from the hands. There is a sweep of horrible music as bits of hair are blown over the desert. Also I see a proud cruel contemptuous captain with a smug grin of satisfaction on his righteous face."

B. "Painting her face. Bette Davis painting her face. Why did they ever call that movie Jezebel? But she didn't paint her face in the movie, did she? Gad, but she was a bitch in that—peace, peace, why do they always talk about peace—it reminds me of a joke I heard—of course she didn't mean that—dead. A burial—a coffin gilded, in gold, with a crown on top—what a word coffin—skull, skull, bones, what an empty picture—skulls lying in an empty case buried in the sand—dogs eating—huge Great Dane with fiery eyes tearing flesh—green fields all around—utter quiet—only the noise of dogs lapping as they eat."

C. "I envisaged a sun swept court, covered with flagstones. Vines covered the surrounding walls of the court, the entrance to which was sufficiently broad to allow the entry of a chariot. I saw a dark man dressed in Roman finery enter and bark a command. Then over the parapet of a balcony, a screaming woman is cast. The chariot ground her under its wheels. The dust settled. I had seen most of this before in the movie, Ben Hur."

D. "This story is a castration-symbol."

E. "I am reminded of the Dean of Women."

When there is such divergence of response to fairly simple statements, the differences in response to more obscure and allusive writing must be immense. Some critics speak of a "total response," as if there always remained a kind of analyzable residue of meaning when the volatile elements have been boiled away. But there is no general or universal response to any poem or statement. There is my response and yours. Both depend on what has happened to me and to you right up to the moment we read the poem. And both responses will have changed when next we read it; for both you and I will have changed. Yet the closer the reader's experience to the writer's, the more nearly will the reader respond. To illustrate:

On September 19, 1819, John Keats wrote a poem beginning

Season of mist and mellow fruitfulness,
Close bosom-friend of the maturing sun!

He called the poem "To Autumn." The autumn had touched him profoundly: the gray dampness of a September morning, the yellow warmth of the midday sun, the scent of the late corn, the smooth fur of the new hazelnut, the sticky hum of bees, all the countless impressions of a fine autumn day in the country. Keats tries to express them in such a way that when we hear that poem our sensitive areas light up, and we receive an inward impression akin to his; but *akin* not identical, and farther or nearer as our experiences of autumn have been nearer or remoter from his.

Autumn in England and in the northern United States is very similar. Unless the hearer has been wholly conditioned to city life and never moves away from its streets, the poem is likely to affect him in much the same way as Keats was affected.

But take the "Ode to a Nightingale." Here the central experience (out of which that poem was conceived) was the song of a nightingale heard in Hampstead on a warm night in mid-May. There are no nightingales in the northern states, and therefore we lack that direct emotional response to the song of the nightingale, one of the most moving of bird songs, for she chooses to sing at midnight and in the early hours, a most plaintive song. Small wonder that the poets from Sophocles onward have hymned her art. That song must first have been heard before the poem will light up the larger areas of a reader's sensitivity. He receives much if he uses his imagination, but far more if the nightingale's song has been part of his experience.

A poem is nothing but silent marks on paper until it causes something to happen in the mind of the reader; it is an ignition key, a dead thing in itself, but yet a record of the poet's emotion and the cause of the hearer's.

But on this view there are two opposing schools of thought. One holds that the poet's purpose is not merely to express himself, but so to express himself that his poem evokes a passion akin to his own. Others hold that the poetic—indeed all art—is but self-expression, the artist giving utterance to that which is within him without a thought for any observer or hearer. If the observer can understand, so; but if not, he is one of the uninitiated. Hence that extreme kind of art wherein the artist, as it were, gorges himself on paint or words and throws up on the carpet to the great relief of his overclogged psyche. Results may reveal to the trained observer the contents of the maw; but it is chaos or worse to the humbler catechumen.

The first meaning of "literature" is thus "human communication recorded in words." Its nature depends on the writer and what he is trying to communicate; for human nature has two sides, denoted by such words as *body* merged with *soul, reason* contrasted with *imagination, perception* contrasted with *sensation* (which Jung defines as "perception through conscious sensory processes") and *intuition* ("perception by way of unconscious contents and connections").

This pronouncement is no new discovery but a confirmation

from an empiric psychologist of what writers and critics have known since Aristotle and Longinus.

Each of the two sides of human nature has its own method of expression in words: *prose* and *poetry*. *Prose* is the method of rational expression, *poetry* of intuition, sensation and feeling. Both words have, however, become overused and worn, as the lexicographers reveal. Dr. Johnson is, as always, illuminating—and exasperating: "*Poet:* An inventor; an author of fiction; a writer of poems; one who writes in measures. *Poetaster:* A vile petty poet. *Poetess:* a she poet. *Poetry:* 1. Metrical Composition; the art or practice of writing poems. *Poems:* Poetical pieces."

The Shorter Oxford English Dictionary is more generous. Its *Poet* is "a writer in verse (or sometimes elevated prose) distinguished by imaginative power, insight, sensibility, and faculty of expression." Whilst *Poetry* is "the expression of beautiful or elevated thought, imagination, or feeling, in appropriate language, such language containing a rhythmical element and having usually a metrical form."

Poetry is more than these definitions allow. It has *form, method* and *function*. The *form* of poetry includes all those matters considered in prosody—meter, rhyme, stanza, assonance, alliteration, epic, sonnet, and the rest. The *method* of poetry includes the uses of rhythm, imagery, symbol, simile, metaphor, association. The *function* of poetry is to communicate sensation, intuition and feeling. Perhaps the best definition of poetry is that student's who said, "Poetry is just a way of saying something that can't be said otherways." And the poet writes in meter to force his readers to re-create the sounds of his words as he wishes them to be heard.

Critics and historians of literature have diverse means of grouping and identifying poems: by periods, by kinds, by forms, by methods. Another way I have found more effective: to classify poems by *depths*. Some poems are almost wholly on the *surface;* some are *subsoil*—partly on the surface yet communicating largely to and from the subconscious; some are wholly in *depths.*

In taking these terms from the psychologist, we must be morbidly aware that the words "surface," "subsoil" and "depth" are themselves images and symbols. As symbols they touch certain spots which light up others. "Subsoil" suggests something beneath the conscious, something below the floor, or roots piercing down, or the base of the iceberg below the waves; and the iceberg itself is a common image in psychology. "Depths" also suggests the soil beneath the oak, the water below the iceberg; but "depth" connotes darkness, and darkness is often impregnated with evil; there is no necessary notion of evil in depth psychology. Contrariwise, darkness can also connote a state of holiness, as in the "dark night of the soul" or Vaughan's poem "The Night." Verbal images, especially when used as scientific concepts, are so dangerous and elusive; they ricochet uncontrollably. We can too easily be trammeled in an image and then deceive ourselves that "subconscious" and "depth" have an actual existence; there is no physical area wherein the subconscious lurks.

In a *surface poem* the expression is direct; its full meaning is immediately clear at first reading. A simple lyric, "Who is Sylvia?" is a surface poem, a plain statement; though even the simplest statements often evoke sensations because of the incontrollable connotations of words. Herrick's poetry is usually "surface," and not the worse for that.

Much poetry written in the eighteenth century is also of the surface, the directest of statements. Some indeed question whether such a work as the *Essay on Criticism* can even be called poetry; is it not rational statement directed solely to the intellect? The answer depends on whether anything is added to the statement by the use of poetic form. Thus:

Those rules of old, discovered, not devised,
Are Nature still, but Nature methodized;
Nature, like Liberty, is but restrained
By the same laws which first herself ordained.

The statement, paraphrased in the looser expression of prose, immediately loses something because the form of poetry—meter, stress, order—have given some pleasure to the sensations added to the intellectual delight caused by the comprehension of the statement itself. To that extent Pope's *Essay* is poetry, though its content could more naturally be expressed in prose—by anyone else.

In dividing poetry into *surface, subsoil* and *depth* there is no suggestion of quality. A good surface poem is far more satisfying than a poor depth poem. Nor should these or any critical terms ever be rigidly applied; they are like the primary colors in the rainbow—red and yellow and blue, but no distinguishable point at which yellow merges into orange, or orange passes into red. The difference between the kinds is rather a matter of degree, merely of general convenience of description.

In a *subsoil poem* there is statement, clear in itself, but yet causing echoes and vibrations of sensation and intuition. Thus Shakespeare:

That time of year thou mayst in me behold
When yellow leaves, or none, or few, do hang
Upon those boughs which shake against the cold,
Bare ruined choirs where late the sweet birds sang.

The surface meaning is simple: I am declining, I grow old. The *form* is the common sonnet pattern. The *method* employs the oblique statement through familiar images of yellow leaves, ruined choirs, bird song now silent. But the images reverberate. The last "leaves" suggest the chilly damp of early November, and the reader's own intuitions (mostly subconscious) of the declining year. "Bare ruined choirs" is an image which lights many sensitive spots, for the word "choir" itself has two meanings, both present—the singers, and the place in the chancel where they sang; and the memory of spoliation and destruction and neglect, and a gracious way of life now gone; and the image of roofless abbeys, blended with the picture of an avenue of leafless trees whose upper branches meet and intertwine, and the birds which sang there in April. Each image in turn stirs and creates other images and nostalgic memories.

Depth poetry is much favored by modern poets, though it is not entirely a modern kind, for many poets of the seventeenth century wrote in this way. In a depth poem the statement is far from obvious, and its meanings—even its surface or subsoil meanings—are often disputed by critics who are expert in the interpretation of this kind. Thus one of the simpler sections (IV) of T. S. Eliot's famous poem *The Waste Land* runs:

> *Phlebas the Phoenician, a fortnight dead,*
> *Forgot the cry of gulls, and the deep sea swell*
> *And the profit and loss.*
>   *A current under sea*
> *Picked his bones in whispers. As he rose and fell*
> *He passed the stages of his age and youth*
> *Entering the whirlpool.*
>   *Gentile or Jew*
> *O you who turn the wheel and look to windward,*
> *Consider Phlebas, who was once handsome and*
>   *tall as you.*

Elizabeth Drew annotates: "Critics differ in the interpretation of this section. Some see the description as that of actual death; others as that of the surrender to the sacrificial death, or the initiation ritual, as a prelude to rebirth. The latter seems more probable. Phlebas is the symbol of the drowned fertility god who will rise again, and the condition described seems to be that 'freedom from attachment' which the Fire Sermon demanded." The meaning of such depth poetry cannot be translated into prose; it can only be felt by those readers whose experience (which includes their reading) has coincided with the author's own deepest intuitions.

The ultimate distinction between *poetry* and *prose* is clear. Since the function of prose is to communicate with the intellect, the purest prose is on the surface; its statements are complete in themselves. When prose has its subsoils and depths, it ceases to be pure prose and to some extent takes over the forms and functions of poetry. No exact demarcation between prose and poetry can be drawn, for there is hardly any prose which lacks all appeal to sensation and intuition because of the nature of the words which it uses. A proposition in Euclid comes near to being pure prose; yet even here mystics and mathematicians can achieve deep experiences from contemplating a straight line, a circle or an equilateral triangle; all of which can be symbols of the profoundest metaphysical truths.

For general purposes *prose* is normal speech. To become literature prose must first be recorded in writing. Since prose includes all kinds of written statement from the Apocalypse to a handbill, any attempt at categorizing must be arbitrary. Nevertheless most kinds of prose can be included in three main groups: *prose of record, prose of instruction,* and *prose of delight* or *entertainment.* Naturally the best specimens of prose of record and prose of instruction will also be prose of delight.

Prose of record includes all kinds of writing where the author is recording something that it may be remembered or conveyed as information to a reader. This category includes history, diaries, letters, biography, newspapers and journals, reports, memoranda, agreements and the like. There is also a considerable area which is both "record" and "instruction."

Prose of instruction includes works of science, philosophy, religion, textbooks and manuals, laws, regulations, any writing which is primarily intended to teach. It can also include works of criticism.

Prose of delight includes novels, romances, short stories and essays, some works of criticism, and all other kinds of writing where the writer's prime purpose is to entertain. All fiction is prose of delight—at least that is presumably the author's intention—from the lowest thriller to the highest efforts of the Russian novelists. Students of literature will be chiefly concerned with prose of this group, but not solely, because any work of record or of instruction can also give delight. The letters of Keats were originally written for individual recipients but they still cause the widest delight; and who would have thought that when the Reverend James Smith of St. John's College, Cambridge, began to decipher certain manuscript volumes in the library of Magdalene College he would reveal the most remarkable record of a human being ever compiled? Whatever the bounds of literary prose, Samuel Pepys' Diary is certainly in the highest degree prose of entertainment, record and instruction.

Poetry, though mainly the province of the student of literature, belongs also to the musicians, for many poems, especially lyric, were originally intended to be sung. Some were even written alongside the music. Thomas Campion, for instance, was an expert in both forms of composition. In his *Two Books of Airs* he wrote: "I have chiefly aimed to couple my words and notes lovingly together; which will be much for him to do that hath not power of both."

Similarly in drama, actors and students of literature have each a half-share, for the drama is written for the stage. The words spoken are only a part of the whole production. A dramatist is essential to the making of the play, but so also are the actors; and many successful and even great dramas have been written for particular actors, including some of Shakespeare's. For a drama to become literature, the playscript must be finely written. The final test whether any play owes more to the actors than to the author lies in its readability. Good actors can make a success of a poorly written play; only a well-written play can survive the test of silent critical reading. The study of drama thus requires a special and different attitude from the reader, who must be his own director of a performance played on the stage of his imagination.

Out of all these different kinds of writing and their study emerge certain principles, purposes and results. Francis Bacon saw them long ago, and he summed them up in the opening sentence of his essay "Of Studies": "Studies serve for delight, for ornament, and for ability." This is true of the study of literature.

We may read for instruction and knowledge, or to pass a competitive examination, that is, for "ability." When so, we are more concerned with what the writer is telling us and less with his manner of telling.

We may read for "ornament" to improve our social graces, and to furnish us with apt quotations and matter for elegant conversation: a useful achievement. The rough diamond has its price; but the polished kind are more pleasing to the eye, and commercially more valuable. A man whose descriptive vocabulary is limited to "swell" and "lousy" lacks a certain distinction of manner, which is a social handicap; he probably also lacks a sensitive and perceptive mind.

But the chief reason for reading is "delight." Further, "delight" is the quality which distinguishes "literature" from other kinds of writing. The study of literature is thus a form of pleasure; and that writing which does not give pleasure (whatever else it may give by way of instruction or edification) is not "literature."

The former definition of literature can now be expanded: "Literature is a means of evoking pleasure in a reader by written words."

For the experience of literature, the reader is as essential as the writer. Good writers can only flourish when there are good readers; without encouragement even a genius soon wilts. It is a historical fact that most great English writers have been appreciated by their contemporaries provided that they lived to a normal age and that their works were generally available. Some certainly have had to wait for a long time, especially originators of new modes, such as Wordsworth, Shelley, or T. S. Eliot. The one major exception is William Blake, who was not recognized during his long life; but that was hardly the fault of the public, for Blake issued his best work in editions of about twenty copies, hand engraved and tinted, at £5 to £20 apiece.

The good reader needs two qualities. He must take both pleasure and pains in his reading. But all serious pleasure demands effort. Angling is a poor sport until the angler has learned to manage his tackle and has achieved a knowledge of wind and water and of the habits of fish. And so with other activities, swimming, for instance. They do not become pleasures until the participant has taken great pains.

Reading is an arduous pleasure of the mind; and to gain the greatest pleasure from good writing, the reader must take pain to prepare himself by study. He needs some knowledge of the elements of the art of writing and of the use of language; form, words, metaphor, image, prosody and verse, and even grammar, the kinds and types of poem, and in some measure the relation of one work to another in time and in kind. The reading of Lyly's *Euphues* is not, for most readers, an exciting pleasure, though it is more lively than is realized by those who have known it only from brief extracts in a survey textbook. But once *Euphues* has been read, the reader understands something of the tastes of its first readers, and of the conversation of Falstaff. Nor again is William Godwin's *Enquiry Concerning Political Justice and Its Influence on Morals and Happiness* light reading for a summer afternoon; but once read, Shelley becomes much more intelligible both as a poet and a man. Shelley was so excited by *Political Justice* that he sought out Godwin, and ran away with Godwin's daughter.

A good reader needs zeal as well as zest. He becomes catholic in his reading and his tastes; he does not confine himself to any one kind of writing. He reads Herrick as well as Donne. He can pass with enjoyment from *The Idylls of the King* to *Tristram Shandy,* from *Songs of Innocence* to *Don Juan,* from *Urn Burial* to *Alice in Wonderland.* He shares in a thousand experiences and in so doing he widens his mind and his horizons. He develops a critical instinct to discriminate between good and bad writing, between vivid and drab experience, even if he cannot always analyze his own reasons. He also realizes that reading is not a substitute for life but a comment on life; and that life is not—as one might gather from some modern commentators—only excusable because it provides matter for artists.

The well-read man fortifies his reading with experience, and by reading intensifies and enriches his own experience. He learns from Lear to make proper arrangements for his old age, from Capulet and Polonius not to interfere in his daughter's love affairs, and from Jepthah to refrain from rash promises, even to God.

The good reader—Dr. Johnson called him the *common reader*—is not usually himself a writer of books or a professional critic. He keeps his amateur status. Professional readers, be they scholars or critics, may have read more and be more expert in analyzing what they read, but the life of a book depends on the pleasure that it gives common readers, who are not the judges of a book but the jury. And it depends on the verdict of the jury, not on the learning of the judge, whether the accused is jailed or acquitted.

Professional readers are quite severely handicapped, for they are under the curse of their calling. Too soon and too easily they lose the ability to enjoy common things. They pass judgments by the rules of the profession; they suffer from the jealousy of their rivals; and too often they have lost the sense of wonder. Whenever they read a book, it is not to enjoy but to analyze, to evaluate, and to pontificate.

The common reader is not easily identified, for he is beyond the reach of a questionnaire. Booksellers know him well; he keeps them alive, even if he browses long and often before buying a book. Professionals are of less use to the bookseller; we get so many of our books free. Without the common reader publishers too would go out of business. Nor should critics ever forget, especially in their more exalted moments, the crude fact that a book is not only a work of art but also an article of sale.

The publisher receives too little credit for his part in the existence of literature; for he, not the critic, is the midwife of a book. Such is the ingratitude, or snobbery, or stupidity of historians of literature that they seldom, if ever, include even the names of publishers in their histories, although men of letters owe everything to them—their existence, their fame, and their income. Unless a publisher is first willing to show his faith in a writer by risking his own money, even a Milton remains to the end mute and inglorious. *Paradise Lost* survives because a publisher once paid £10 for the manuscript and contracted for its printing.

Nor does the fame only of contemporary writers depend on the publishers. But for enterprising publishers, some even of the greatest of writers of the past would have remained unread. The poems of John Donne are today the most popular relics of the early seventeenth century. In his own generation Donne was notorious for original ways of expressing himself. His poems were first printed after his death in 1631; at that time Donne was in high favor with the younger poets, as Carew's "Elegy upon the death of Dr. Donne" records. The poems were reprinted four times by 1669, but not again until 1779 (in Bell's edition of English poets). Nearly a century later Grosart included Donne in the Fuller Worthies Library—a series of rare texts limited to 100 copies, for collectors only. In 1895 Donne's poems were again issued as a rarity for the Grolier Club. But the next year Grant Richards boldly ventured in including Donne, together with Herrick, Campion, Vaughan and others, in the Muses Library, a series intended to popularize the Elizabethan and Jacobean poets. Sixteen years later H. J. C. Grierson produced a scholarly edition of all Donne's poems so that the literary-minded could now read him with more intelligence. Donne thus became available for the younger generation of revolutionary poets revolting against the last of the romantics; and ever since, Donne has been regarded as the Second English Poet.

In so praising publishers, we need not romanticize them; usually they have their reward on earth.

To return to the common reader. He may be defined as one who reads with zest, discrimination and taste not for professional advantage but for sheer pleasure. He has enough experience of life to be able to share in the record of other experiences, both common and uncommon, enough artistic experience to appreciate good art, and enough common sense not to be deceived by shams all the time. One aspect of the serious study of literature will be to trace the likes of the common reader.

In this examination we soon find that certain books and authors achieve a kind of permanence but that others, although they may enjoy far greater vogue for a time, pass out of sight and disappear, if not permanently, at least for a long time—as happened to Donne. To survive, a book must possess a peculiar quality that enables it, generation after generation, to cause delight. But this delight will be different for each generation. The qualities in *Hamlet* admired by the most modern critics are not the same as those admired by A. C. Bradley, or by Matthew Arnold, or by Coleridge, or by Dr. Johnson, or by Pope, or by Dryden, or by Gabriel Harvey. As Dr. Johnson so grandiloquently put it:

> Nothing can please many, and please long, but just representations of general nature. Particular manners can be known to few, and therefore few only can judge how nearly they are copied. The irregular combinations of fanciful invention may delight awhile, by that novelty of which the common satiety of life sends us all in quest; but the pleasures of sudden wonder are soon exhausted, and the mind can only repose on the stability of truth.

Hamlet is a supreme example of what "pleases many and pleases long." But lay *Hamlet* alongside *The Spanish Tragedy*, an even more popular play in its own generation. Some modern students of drama read it; very occasionally dramatic societies perform it; and the general verdict is "how crude!

how ridiculous!" *Hamlet* has thus a reflective power to give pleasure to successive generations of readers. We look into the mirror and we see ourselves there. This quality exists in all permanent works of art; it is usually called *universality*.

While universality is abundantly present in *Hamlet, The Spanish Tragedy* lacks it. This is no more than recognizing a fact; we cannot—seemingly—analyze universality. If we could, we should know its essence. Professional critics would then be able to bet on certainties, and to say of any new work "this will still be readable fifty, or even a hundred, years hence." And notoriously they cannot. The history of criticism abounds in the confident errors of even the greatest critics. Francis Jeffrey, the *Edinburgh Review*er, one of the shrewdest of the critics of the nineteenth century, one of the few who wrote sensibly and sympathetically of the work of Keats and Wordsworth when it was new from the press, in October 1829 ventured a prophecy. He lamented that the great reputations of the 1820's—Wordsworth, Shelley, Southey, Keats, Crabbe and the rest—were already faded things of the past; yet there did seem to be one writer whose work was likely to survive—Felicia Hemans, a lady who in poetic stature nowadays ranks with Ella Wheeler Wilcox and Edgar Guest.

Certain kinds of writing are more likely to be universal. They must possess two qualities: they must treat of those matters which cause the largest areas of sensitive spots to glow, that is, which concern every man—life, love, death, unaltering nature, man, woman, and God; and they must also be written in a universal and not a local language, comprehensible to the common reader. This was the truth after which Matthew Arnold was groping when he produced his samples of what he regarded as "high seriousness." Yet high seriousness is not necessary to universal literature, which is not concerned with any one level of feeling, thought or emotion. There are universal levities as well as universal profundities. If Sophocles is still profoundly moving, Aristophanes is still embarrassingly funny.

Greatness in literature is not solely a matter of longevity, though we must recognize greatness in a work which has endured for generations. Survival for a century used to be regarded as the mark of a classic; survival for longer is surely a mark of genius, which we may regard according to our lights as luck or a gift of Grace. Whatever it is, the quality of greatness lies outside scientific investigation. We cannot explain; we can only record.

Nor are the works which possess this permanence those which necessarily please most. We are far more quickly and sometimes deeply moved by that which will soon die: by the intimate sonnet which only you and I understand; or—on a lower level—by the campus joke which will be meaningless two weeks hence.

Actually, the closer the expression comes to the immediate moment, the deeper will be the feeling and the response; but the sooner will they fade. For this reason much of the finest writing, poetry and prose, of the present generation will not and cannot last, because our best writers are concerned with analyzing our world for us and in a solely contemporary idiom. Fifty, even twenty years hence, that world will have so changed that the analysis will have become meaningless. The world so accurately pictured in *The Forsyte Saga* or *The World of William Clissold* is already dead; and the most brilliant of Shaw's comedies of contemporary life must now be played as costume pieces.

II. ENGLISH

The second key word to be defined is *English*. In speaking of English literature it is too often assumed that "English" means written in the dialect spoken and understood by inhabitants of Great Britain, Ireland, the United States of America, Canada, Australia and certain other parts of the world. "English" as applied to literature has a far narrower significance. As it is now customary and reasonable to regard American, Canadian and Australian literature as distinct kinds, so English literature is written by and for persons living not in Great Britain but in England. The English, as is often forgotten, are a people quite different from the Scots, the Irish and the Welsh (all of whom doubtless murmur "Thank God"). It shows an ignorance of the essential fact to speak of their literature as "British" as if there was considerable admixture of Irish, Scottish and Welsh writings, which are in fact hardly enough either in quantity or quality to give any perceptible taste to the brew.

English literature implies that the author is dealing with facts and notions that form common areas of sensitive spots to English men and women. Thus the nature poetry of the English—and they have a powerful instinct for nature—is concerned with the facts of their own countryside; with primroses which appear in the hedgerows in March, with wild daffodils that come before the swallow dares, with cowslips in April, bluebells in May, with the thrush and the blackbird and the robin (a cocky little bird, very different from what is called a robin in America, which is indeed a kind of thrush), with wild roses in June, with green meadows. This English way of life and its literature, indefinable but distinct, has been continuous for forty and more generations. It has a deep sense of the past lacking in newer civilizations. In nearly every English village there is a church at least five hundred, sometimes a thousand, years old, and houses that have been inhabited continuously for two, three, even four hundred years. The student does not learn about these things from books, museums or even pictures; he can only absorb them by contact.

The English have also been conditioned by their system of education. Since the Second World War there have been many changes but even now most of the old prejudices and customs survive. There was (and still is) a social cleavage between those who can afford to pay for the education of their children and those who accept what the State provides. In the early decades of the twentieth century, the State gathered a child into the elementary school at the age of five and turned him out at fourteen either to work for his living or to become an apprentice or to enter a secondary or grammar school. Here he was prepared for the School Certificate, which he took usually at the age of sixteen. This certificate was awarded after an examination in half a dozen basic subjects and conducted by one of the universities. Schools were grouped into areas and all pupils from the different schools sat for the same examination. There was thus keen competition between schools, and much cramming, for the competence of the teaching was reflected in the number of certificates gained by the school. The School Certificate was a kind of magic seal. Employers accepted it as a proof of mental attainment; the universities demanded it as a test of fitness for admission. After taking the School Certificate most pupils left the secondary school; only the best stayed on to be prepared for a university. The proportion of those who enter universities in England is far less than in the United States.

Those who can afford to pay fees send their children to other kinds of schools. It is a heavy, often excessive burden, but demanded by custom, prestige and the obvious advantages to the child.

At the age of four or four and a half, children of the feepayers are sent to a nursery school where they learn the elements of reading, writing, arithmetic and other accomplishments until seven or eight. Thereafter the sexes are separated until they come together again ten years later at the university. From the nursery school small boys pass into a preparatory school which prepares them for entry to one of the public schools. Preparatory schools are small, varying from about thirty to 120 boys. They are private ventures, run for the profit (sometimes considerable) of their owners, but not the worse for that, because there is great competition between schools, whose success depends on results.

Thirty and more years ago, when modern writers of the older generation were small boys, the training and routine were narrow and strict; and they acquired some useful (and some worthless) scholarly equipment. They learned the elements of Latin (sometimes also Greek), French, English history, Scripture, geography, arithmetic, geometry, spelling, essay writing and composition and a little literature; music and drawing were "extras." Much of the training was arid and mechanical. Latin was largely a matter of grammatical rules and exceptions, and the translation of English sentences into Latin, with a rigid insistence on accuracy. They learned also by rote the dates of the Kings of England from William the Conqueror (1066-1087) to George the Fifth; the kings of Israel and Judah; the twelve tribes and their location on the map of Palestine; and the journeys of St. Paul (also mapped). At the end of five or six years at his preparatory school a boy had thus imbibed considerable quantities of Latin grammar and syntax, a knowledge of Latin and Greek irregular verbs, the functioning of nouns and their genders and the numerous exceptions, but also he had been introduced to classical literature in the form of selections from Caesar, Ovid and Xenophon.

The daily routine was strenuous for a small boy. School began at 9:00 and classwork continued till 1:00. Then dinner, followed by an hour or more of compulsory games for all—football in the winter, cricket and swimming in the summer. From 4:00 to 6:00 more classwork, followed by tea, and then a period of an hour or more of preparation for the next day. This was the routine for four days a week; on Wednesday and Saturday there was no afternoon schoolwork, but games lasted longer.

This routine lasted from mid-September to mid-December. A month's holiday followed. The second term ran to the beginning of April, followed by another month's holiday; and so through to the end of July, with a summer holiday of seven weeks. This division of the year is general in the English school system.

The preparatory schools prepare their boys for the "common entrance," a qualifying examination which admitted them to a public school, but the brightest are coached to compete for entrance scholarships, awarded for merit, not need.

Modern educationists would doubtless tremble with horror at such pedagogic barbarity. But yet, the most valuable lessons I learned in earlier school days were those which I was compelled to learn by threats—and not only threats—of punishment, and those which I learned by myself without the help or guidance of any teacher. Knowledge of chronology is the first essential in understanding the past, and an English boy who knows his "Kings" has already been provided with a framework into which he can thereafter fit any historical fact, be it a person, battle, enactment, play or poem. Nor can Latin grammar ever be exciting to any normal boy, but it is essential knowledge for later study.

An elementary truth in education, too often forgotten, is that today's lesson may not bear its fruit for another ten years, which is a chief reason why a child or even a sophomore is incapable of regulating his own syllabus.

At the age of thirteen to fourteen the boy leaves his preparatory school and enters a public school.

Few Americans understand or can even imagine an English public school. In the eyes of the law the public schools are charitable institutions to promote education; but they are in no sense "public." They admit only the sons of parents who can pay the high fees, and, in some schools, of fathers who are technically "gentlemen," that is, either have an independent income or belong to certain professions. The English tradition is to educate boys and girls at separate schools where boys are taught by men and girls by women. There are also many public schools for girls, modeled on the traditions of the schools for boys; but that system is not always so successful, since the mistresses, usually devoted spinsters, often discourage the feminine and domestic virtues and instill their charges, rather, with the more masculine and intellectual attainments.

There are about 130 public schools for boys, varying in size from Eton, with over a thousand, to the small schools with about 150. The average is about 350 boys, which is the right size, for in such a school everyone, masters and boys, can know at least the names of everyone else. In too large a school identities are lost and in a smaller school there are too few for proper competition.

The best public schools are largely, if not wholly, for boarders. It is an essential part of the system that boys shall leave home and live at school. This has been a tradition since the Middle Ages, when the sons and daughters of good family were sent to be pages or waiting gentlewomen in great houses where they learned good manners and the management of a household.

This English custom of the "privileged" of discarding their offspring at so tender an age seems heartless to those who have never experienced it. "How bitter," they cry, "must be the sufferings of a sensitive child, torn from its parents and thrust alone into a strange school." In truth, among English parents there is considerable disagreement. Those who were themselves unhappy at school keep their children at home; those who look back with satisfaction to their own days at a public school make great sacrifices to give the same advantages to their own children. The justification lies in the results, about which it is impossible to dogmatize.

The theory is that a boy will be better taught not only in the classroom but also to face reality in a hard world if separated from his parents for eight and a half months in the year, and that love between child and parents is ultimately greater—not less—than if he remained at home afflicted by the daily division of allegiance between parent and teacher. Certainly in many homes there are tears at the end of the holidays, but counterbalancing joy at the end of the school term. In this, as in all theories of education, the prime principle must be the final result. The worst possible kind of education is that which sacrifices the ultimate good of the child to sparing it from immediate discomfort or pain.

If education is to be a training for adult life (as presumably pedagogic experts would agree) it is more important for the child to learn early that sane living includes the cheerful endurance of drudgery, frustration and social conformity than that it become expert in square dancing and baton twirling.

Each year in the third week of September, hundreds of small boys of thirteen or thereabouts are for the first time decanted into a strange school. Each school has its own peculiar organization, but normally it is divided into houses, each house holding thirty to fifty boys.

The new boy is soon confronted by the prefects. In each house a senior boy is head of the house, aided by prefects and house prefects, senior boys with considerable authority. They are responsible for most of the discipline and organization outside schoolwork, and they have powers to punish summarily. In a good house the prefects and house master work together, as the company commander and the sergeants do in a good regiment. The new boy is expected to behave with due humility, and if too prone to exhibit his individuality, public opinion crudely tames him. He sleeps in a dormitory with a dozen or more others, and shares an austere room with lockers for his private treasures. Here he spends his small leisure, but for the first two or three years he will not have much leisure.

In a house, relations between house master and boys are governed by curious unwritten customs. A perpetual warfare between authority and original sin is normal. A small boy naturally tries to be idle, or wanders out of bounds, or eats unwholesome things at unauthorized times; if he is utterly depraved he will even smoke cigarettes. If he is undetected, he wins; if caught, he is punished, and there an end; there is no malice on either side. Most schoolboys used to regard a beating as a reasonable way of settling major differences between the individual and the law, and the bottom as the natural place of beating. It was a mark of fortitude to accept such punishment without tears. Such at least was the norm earlier in the century, though since then the psychologists have made their protests and bodily punishment is less frequent. In later years a complete and lasting friendship between boy and house master is not uncommon; and in the major crises of early manhood a young man often turns to his house master as a natural guide.

The first year is the worst for the small boy; but he soon gears into the system and grows a protective skin against the pricks of society. By the end of the first year he has learned the meaning of discipline and how to be one of the crowd; this faculty is sometimes called the community spirit.

As the boy grows more senior, in his third or fourth year, he is promoted to a study. Now he leaves the society of his house room to share a small cell with three or four others. He is no longer constantly supervised and he can, in a way, express himself, for his study is his workroom and playroom.

As the next step in his progress, he is promoted to house prefect. This stage is a severe test of character and personality. He has authority over others, but only within his own house. If he survives this testing period successfully, he is promoted to school prefect and becomes one of the aristocracy of the school. As a prefect he enjoys many privileges; he is independent of most minor rules; but he has many duties and responsibilities; and he becomes a Great Man in the eyes of small boys. Again, it is a test of character whether he is fit to have power. When the prefects are good and conscientious, a school runs easily and smoothly; when they are bad, a school quickly declines. In a good house and school, prefects, house masters and headmaster work harmoniously with a common object.

The final peak of a boy's ambition is to be head of the school. He is a glorious being, almost as important as a regimental master sergeant.

For schoolwork all boys from each house combine. They

are organized into "forms" (not "classes"), and usually the top form is called the sixth. Each form has its own form master (not "teacher"), who supervises generally and watches the progress of each boy, but for particular subjects there are specialist masters. In lower forms the common number is twenty-five, rarely more than thirty. In the form room discipline in theory is strict; but it depends on the personality of the master. The man who can keep good discipline is respected; the inefficient is despised and ragged. It is assumed as a matter of common experience that most small boys—up to fifteen or so—are averse to work and must therefore be pressured. If he does not respond, the boy is made to repeat his assigned work in his own small leisure; in extreme cases he is beaten. This atmosphere lasts however only while the boy remains in the colt stage. As he grows up the attitude of authority changes.

When the boy reaches Fifth Form he will be preparing for the School Certificate, which at the public schools was usually taken at fifteen and a half to sixteen. Once past that barrier his real education begins. The next stage is the Higher Certificate (which may give him a State scholarship at the university). He passes into the Sixth Form: classical, modern languages, or science. He now specializes as he is coached for one of the professional examinations or to compete for an open scholarship at one of the universities.

A Sixth Form is quite small: ten or fewer boys who come under the care of an expert, the Sixth Form master, a scholar or scientist of high academic standing. The boy is now a responsible being, working in partnership, and no longer in opposition to his master. The value of what a boy can receive from a good Sixth Form master is incalculable, for he is in daily contact with a first-class mind to whom learning is a vocation. Naturally most boys in the Sixth Form are also prefects, for it is usual to find the best minds in a school in the ablest bodies.

In the old classical Sixth Form a boy spent most of his time in the study of Greek and Latin. Each week he turned passages of English prose into imitations of Cicero or Tacitus, Thucydides or Demosthenes, and turned English poetry into hexameters or elegiacs. He learned to translate from Greek and Latin into English and he was encouraged to read for himself in all literatures. By the time he sat for a scholarship at Oxford or Cambridge (at the age of eighteen), he had read widely in the classics and could translate at sight from most authors. He was also expected to be able to express his own opinion on the world around him; daily reading of the best newspapers and weekly journals was a normal part of his intellectual life.

This old-fashioned classical education had its grievous drawbacks. It was narrow; it ignored science; and it bred an intellectual snobbishness; but it had also its practical uses. No one could read the great classics—Homer, Virgil, the Greek tragedians, Thucydides, Herodotus, Xenophon, Livy and Tacitus, Demosthenes and Cicero, Horace, Catullus, Ovid, Juvenal, Martial and Persius and the rest—without, if only by a kind of osmosis, acquiring a wide and varied knowledge of humanity. As a training it lasted in England from Roger Ascham to the First World War. Most writers of note had been molded by it, and in the eighteenth and nineteenth centuries every public speaker could tag his speeches with an apt quotation familiar to his audience. Even for such professions as the law and the civil service it was considered a good preparation because it developed a well-stocked mind which had encountered, at least in reading, most kinds of human situations. No teacher of English can ignore it, for without some classical training he will miss most of the nuances in any writer before Bernard Shaw.

The classical training has its wider uses. Anyone grounded in Latin grammar has a valuable standard for contrast and comparison, as I found even in learning Urdu. Once my Latin gained me a temporary and undeserved reputation as a linguist. A party of officers was traveling by train from Taranto to Havre and we wished to supplement wartime rations. I accosted a likely Italian, and guessing that *ovum* probably had a near modern equivalent, I tried *ovio*. He looked blankly. Then light dawned and he cried out: "Ha! *uovvi, uovvi!"*; and eggs appeared. At night our compartment was unlit, and I tried again. I pointed to the light and exclaimed *"illuminatzione?"*; and there was light. Given great patience and good will on both sides most elementary needs can be communicated without words. I did once buy lamp oil in an Arab bazaar by signs alone, and I had no lamp. And signs can be supplemented by pictures; but not always. In Prague, being advised that goat's flesh was a local delicacy, I tried to convey my desire to the waiter by drawing a goat on the menu. He looked puzzled, and then alarmed—maybe he thought that I was invoking the Devil—and fled to find an "English-sprik."

In practical matters, however, a classical education can sometimes be an embarrassing handicap. At Cambridge I had studied Greek architecture and thought I knew something of building, until I was suddenly called upon to become a master builder. In the summer of 1918, the daily shade temperature in Mesopotamia was a steady 115°. At such times the morale of soldiers declines, for between ten in the morning and the sloping of the sun in the late afternoon there was nothing to do but sweat, talk bawdry, gamble or read. To mitigate this tedium, there went forth an order that each company should build itself a recreation hut. The walls were to be of brick, 30 feet in length, and 15 feet in breadth, and the height thereof to be 7 feet, with a door, and windows on either side, and a roof of palm matting (supplied by the Royal Engineers).

At that time I was in temporary command of a company; now I must turn overseer. Bricks were easy. Each morning a party went down to the riverbank, puddled mud with straw, and passed it through a mold; by evening the bricks were baked hard. But how were bricks to be laid so that the walls of our hut would rise perpendicular and horizontal?

I raked over memories of my education; of the Israelites in Goshen, of Solomon's temple, and Nehemiah, and my Uncle

Frederick Harrison's notes on the Decorated and Perpendicular Styles in Sussex churches, of Balbus that incomparable builder of walls, of Greek temples and their metopes and friezes and architraves, and the three styles of column—Doric, Ionic and Corinthian. None of these helped. And the Latin grammar mocked with an old tag: *Erant muri Babilonii ducenti pedes alti* (an example, I suspect, of apposition). More immediately relevant were the words of the song so often sung on the march:

I bought a load of bricks for to build a chimney high,
I bought a load of bricks for to build a chimney high,
I bought a load of bricks for to build a chimney high,
And the bloody lot fell d o w n—

Very ominous.

So the platoon commanders and the sergeants were summoned. Not one had ever built a recreation hut, not even a pigsty. At last, after diligent search, the Company Sergeant Major produced Private Grover, T., a surly, difficult man. Private Grover in his time played many parts. He had been policeman, and costermonger, and poacher; but he had also for a short while served as mate to a bricklayer. With Grover as overseer, the building grew nightly, like the walls of Boeotian Thebes to the strumming of Amphion's lyre. That episode set me brooding over *lacunae* in a classical education; for the immediate purpose in hand, Private Grover was the better-educated man.

The old classical education is now dead but not because it failed to train a man to use his hands. The grammarians killed it. Too many of them were less interested in the poetry and the humanity than in peculiar uses of the optative, the vagaries of *quin,* and the subtleties of the Homeric dialect. Browning's Old Grammarian was given a tremendous funeral by his students. Marry, he was dead. When they had left him in his grave so loftily lying, one anonymous vandal took out a piece of chalk and wrote on the flat slab VALE TAEDIOSE (of which the vulgar equivalent is "Bye, bye, Boresome"). Browning omitted that apocryphal detail.

However, even members of the Classical Sixth had other interests; there were valuable out-of-school activities in the different societies which encouraged such hobbies as photography, geology, play reading, debating and the rest. Debating was a most useful training; it should be compulsory for anyone who wishes to profess English. But in this, as in most activities, there was no kind of course of instruction. One learned by experience and by imitation how to marshal an argument, and—not less important—how to hit back with the quip spontaneous and the retort devastating, and (above all) to preserve an unruffled temper, under brutal criticism.

A second aspect of school life is the athletic. Small boys naturally adore the local athletes, and in some schools (as in some universities) games are too prominent. It depends on the general tone of the school, and on the wisdom of the headmaster. Service in the Officers Training Corps is often compulsory, so that the boy learns another kind of training and discipline.

The aim of the system is thus not only intellectual training but to develop a sense of responsibility and leadership. As the boy matures, so he is more and more trusted. In the Sixth Form he is expected to work by himself without any kind of supervision for most of the teaching periods—a valuable preparation for when he is turned loose at the university.

Any society which has existed for generations in the same place collects legends and traditions. There is a perpetual reminder of belonging to a community which has continuously produced some great men not unknown to their contemporaries, and that the present also has its responsibilities to its own generation. This attitude is enhanced by lists of honors gained, rows of old photographs of past worthies, by visits of famous Old Boys, and by the many memorials of the illustrious dead.

Certain defects of the public-school system are obvious. The cost is so excessive that the duller sons of wealthier parents enjoy privileges denied to the brighter children of poor parents. The system breeds a sense of social superiority, seldom blatantly expressed but sometimes subtly implied, and galling to those who do not belong. I have yet to meet an Old Etonian who does not somehow convey his background in the first ten minutes of conversation, usually with an oblique reference to "m' tutor." A candidate for appointment is often asked, as his first question, "what was your school?" and the better known the school, the higher his chances, for former public-school men usually hold the best positions and so tend to choose as their juniors those who have received the same kind of training as themselves. There are, moreover, inner snobberies among the public schools. Boys from Eton and Winchester hold themselves superior to boys from Harrow and Marlborough, and so downward by subtle gradations of caste. Yet the formal education given by the secondary schools is often better as is shown in the lists of scholarships won by their boys in open competition. However, the differences between the two systems of education can be too easily exaggerated; and in later life the third-rate, former public-school boy is the more handicapped if he has nothing wherewith to cover his nakedness but an Old School Tie.

A second criticism is that the system is entirely male, almost monastic, and therefore likely to breed homosexuals. In all human herds, there are individuals with perverted habits, and a few determined specimens can contaminate a house or school as quickly as one rotten peach spoils a whole bushel. Experienced and prudent house masters are usually quick to sense any change of tone in their houses. Nor are principals of mixed high schools without their anxieties. In education more is lost than gained by herding boys and girls together in early adolescence. Out of school, dating and going steady are poor substitutes for that natural friendship between boy and boy and man and man which is so seldom known by the young American. And in school, few unmarried women of forty or fifty can inspire a virile adolescent male of sixteen or seventeen with a zeal for the humaner studies. In the study of English literature, it can be disastrous.

A third disadvantage of the system (seldom expressed or realized) is its wastefulness. Only one in three of those who enter a school stay for the full course of five or six years. Those who leave at sixteen, as soon as they have passed the School Certificate, have endured all the disadvantages of a public school and received few of the benefits of a good secondary education; for it is in the last two years—between sixteen and eighteen—that a boy becomes prefect, member of the Sixth Form, the cricket eleven and the football fifteen or sergeant in the Officers Training Corps, whereby he learns certain lessons in study, man management, self-discipline, co-operation and loyalty to an institution.

There is always a danger in loyalty to established institutions; too often it breeds a conventional mind afraid of change or new ideas. But conventional minds are not confined to English public schools. Other systems of education that aim at producing standardized citizens (as farmers raise standardized hogs with identical hams) are even more clogging and frustrating to brilliant and original adolescents.

Such is the English public-school system. Most men, who as boys were normally adaptable and possessed of fair brains and active bodies, look back at their Old School with affection, often with pride and gratitude. But it is not the best place for those who cannot compromise with crude humanity. Nor should the system be judged by the bitter reminiscences of some literary persons who are by nature hypersensitive and egocentric; they would have been as unhappy in any other kind of herd training.

From his public school the Sixth Form boy progressed to one of the two ancient Universities—Oxford or Cambridge (which, being my own Kindly Mother, I know and love better).

For some reason, not hitherto explained by Oxford scholars, the University of Cambridge has nurtured a disproportionate share of great English writers, among them Wyatt, Ascham, Nashe, Greene, Spenser, Marlowe, Campion, Francis Bacon, Waller, Herrick, Cowley, Crashaw, Milton, Pepys, Dryden, Gray, Wordsworth, Coleridge, Byron, Macaulay and Tennyson. Oxford's contribution includes Sidney, Lyly, Raleigh, Lodge, both Vaughans, Thomas Browne, Addison, Johnson, Shelley (ejected after his first term), Southey, Matthew Arnold, Swinburne and A. E. Housman. Both Universities claim John Donne.

The University of Cambridge is very ancient. The famous Dr. Caius declared that it was founded in 539 B.C., but then he was contesting the claims of Oxford, and in such debates Truth is a silent onlooker from the Strangers' Gallery.

To become a member of the University the student must first be admitted to one of the colleges. Each college consists of a master (though at Queens' he is called President), the fellows, a few bachelors of arts, and the undergraduates, divided into scholars and exhibitioners, and "pensioners." At one time there were also sizars—poor students who were educated free in return for performing some of the domestic chores.

A college is an independent body, self-perpetuating, of which the fellows (called also dons) are permanent residents and trustees. They elect to fill vacancies in their own body, they choose the master—C. P. Snow's novel *The Masters* shows the tortuous process—and they select the new undergraduates. The colleges are financed partly from the fees of their undergraduates, but mainly from their own endowments.

The University is composed of all the colleges. The University admits students on matriculation, provides some lectures, examines students at the end of their residence, and awards degrees. The University is governed by a Senate of all doctors and masters of arts whose names are on the University register, presided over by the vice-chancellor; but there is a small inner Council to control Senate business. The vice-chancellor is chosen from the masters of colleges and usually serves for two years. The supreme titular head of the University is the chancellor, elected for life, a man of great eminence in public life.

The University of Cambridge—and Oxford is similarly organized—is thus a self-governing body. It has no permanent University president, no regents, trustees or other outside governors, and no body of enthusiastic influential and interfering alumni, for all masters of arts can vote in the Senate—if they wish to make the journey.

Before the First World War the life of the student was easy and independent. If he lived in college he had two rooms to himself—a bedroom and a study; and he was cared for by a bedmaker—a middle-aged or elderly woman chosen for her homeliness. All dined together in Hall of an evening at long tables together with the fellows, who sat at the high table on the dais, but they ate other meals by themselves in their rooms, and the college provided a daily ration of a small loaf, two inches of butter (a local measurement) and coal for the fire. Colleges varied in size from Trinity, with over 600, to Magdalene with less than ninety. At Queens' there were fifty-five in my year, about 175 students in all. The colleges were too small to provide rooms for everyone, and so about a third lived out in lodgings, but these were licensed and closely supervised by the University. Each man had his two rooms, and his landlady was obliged to report his late comings.

For the young freshman, life at Cambridge can be very heady, especially if hitherto he has lived under strict tutelage at school and at home. The freshman is welcomed, not hazed. Within the first few weeks the second-year men of his college visit him or leave a card. Secretaries of the various college clubs compete to gather him in, and he has many choices. He can row, or play football, or swim, or act, or sing, or debate, or attach himself to one of the religious groups or political parties; or, if socially inclined, he can join one of the sporting clubs and so proclaim himself a gay dog. If he distinguishes himself in his college, he is invited to join one of the larger University clubs where he mingles with some of the younger dons. If his ambitions are political he tries to attract notice at the weekly debates at the Cambridge Union. At first he must wait patiently until he catches the president's eye and is called upon to speak. Having made a favorable impression, he is invited to "speak on the paper," that is, to be one of the four speakers who open a debate, and whose names are publicly announced on printed notices. Thereafter he is a candidate for office, first for the committee, and then for secretary. If elected, he becomes president automatically, for it is a Cambridge custom both at the Union and in most college clubs that the man chosen secretary ascends to the presidency without further election.

Instruction consists of a few lectures—about six hours a week—and a weekly meeting with the tutor. For the rest, the undergraduate reads, or talks, or plays, or idles as he wishes. Lectures are unimportant; no roll of attendance is taken; there are neither assignments, nor grades, nor examinations.

At the end of three years an undergraduate takes his finals—an impressive and heavy written examination. In the old Classical Tripos ("Tripos" being the name for a course of studies leading to honors) fifteen three-hour papers were written. The student's final class or standing is decided by the committee of examiners, and the class gained at this examination places a man for life. If he gets a first class, he is ultimately eligible for most appointments; if a second, his chances are much less; a third class is useless, a handicap rather.

The whole system of education is thus different from the American. It is intended to produce quality, and the competition is fierce. From his preparatory-school days when he first tried for a scholarship at a public school till he finally emerges as a B.A., a man is working under pressure. The final examination must be taken not later than three years from matriculation. If a man is sick or emotionally disturbed at the time of the examination, that is bad luck; but there is no postponement or second attempt. If he fails (not too hopelessly) to reach the third class, he is allowed a pass degree; if sick, he is allowed an *aegrotat* degree. He can call himself B.A. but the label has little value. Moreover, in assessing the class, the examiners judge only from the papers written in the examination; they take no note of a man's record, personal history or past achievements; nor do they admit the pleas of a psychiatrist.

There can be very hard cases. One of the most brilliant men I knew missed his first because his father chose to die during the examination; he got a second, and so was out of the running for university appointment. To those who are accustomed to consider individuals sympathetically and to grade according to circumstances, it may seem a cruel and ruthless system. Yet in athletics (and in war) there is no room for hard cases; nor do we appeal to the referee to overlook a foul because the poor man is having trouble in his sex life; but the standards for the athletic life are, of course, different from the academic.

Having experienced both systems of examination, I would choose the external and objective as the fairer and more satisfactory. It makes for greater, and not less, friendship and cooperation between teacher and student. Both are then allied to defeat an alien examiner; and the teacher himself is on trial, for his ability is revealed in the success of his students. Where, as in the American system, students are examined by their own teacher, it is often more important for them to know the weak spots of the professor than the content of his course. The teacher too has his own difficulties, especially where the class is small; few can maintain a true Rhadamanthine calm. If scrupulous, he can be unjustly severe in his grades; if warmhearted, he finds it difficult not to make allowances for the poor performance of a good student who has private troubles; and he hates to hurt a sensitive student by giving her a D, which is her real standing.

There is thus a complete divergence between English and American theories of university education. Moreover, the proportion of adolescents who graduate at a college or university in America is about five times as large as in England. The English academic system, as I knew it, was intended mainly to train leaders. In the upper forms of the public schools and at the universities, masters and dons were primarily interested in those who would gain a scholarship or a first. In America and in Canada, the exceptional first-class student is regarded rather as a nuisance, especially in his high-school days, because he fails to conform to the pattern. He is forced to jog along at the pace of his intellectual inferiors in the years when his mind should be stimulated and stretched to the utmost.

The best of our American graduates are as good as the best anywhere, but as a result of the educational system, they must endure at least two or three more years of formal schooling before they can take the Ph.D. preliminary examination, which is the final test that (after they have also written a dissertation) they are fit to teach in a university. Few graduates are ready for the "prelim" before the age of twenty-five. The standard required for the English examination for honors at the B.A. stage is higher than the American preliminary to the Ph.D.; it is taken at the age of twenty-one to twenty-two.

Another difference between the two systems is that English schools are less controlled and administered by professional educationists. They are inspected and counseled by such experts, but since the results of the teaching are checked and demonstrated by the success of his pupils at the public examinations, the individual teacher has considerable freedom. Indeed in some schools the man who knows his subject, and how to teach it, is even regarded as more valuable than one who has had greater training in educational method.

A reader who would comprehend the literature of the English needs either an acute imagination or to have lived in England for quite a while; and he does not live in England merely by sojourning in a boardinghouse within a quarter of a mile of the British Museum. He needs to have seen and felt the procession of the seasons in those places where they can be perceived. A scholar can acquire an ornithological knowledge of the peculiar habits of the cuckoo from the *Encyclopaedia Britannica;* he cannot appreciate Wordsworth's excitement at the first cuckoo until he has heard it toward the end of April; and no cuckoos breed in Bloomsbury.

English literature is thus a literature written for English readers by writers conditioned by English ways of life; and it is a geographical fact that most of it has been written within a hundred and fifty miles of London Bridge.

III. STUDY

The third term to be defined is *study.* If we accept the definition of literature as *writing to be enjoyed,* it follows that the purpose of its study is to increase delight. Study of this kind is just serious reading; it does not demand organized courses of instruction. But study as well as much practice is needed for the full enjoyment of any activity. Even college football cannot be appreciated or understood without an acquired knowledge of its complex rules and strategy; without that knowledge, the goings on in the stadium on a Saturday afternoon seem to the foreign or ignorant spectator to be not a game but an elaborate display of primitive folk ritual.

The study of literature is but a barren activity unless the student is already an eager and an educated reader. This education must begin at birth. And even here too there is great difference between the American and English ways of life. American children first see light in the delivery room; most English infants are born not in the hospital but at home in the same bed wherein they were conceived. Symbolically this is as it should be, for normal birth is a natural domestic event, not a surgical operation, though unsentimental obstetricians may advocate the hospital as more hygienic than the bedroom. Yet American cities are thereby the poorer; how rare those interesting plaques on gray houses that announce "Charles Dickens was born here 7th February 1812." Nor again (unlike Englishmen) do American citizens even die at home. Long before the end they are hustled into the local hospital, to the greater convenience of the pathologist and the undertaker; not for them the ultimate tribute of "Here lived and died William Makepeace Thackeray. . . ."

For the first few years the little student is taught mainly by his mother. If he is lucky, from the time he can first talk and understand words she tells him tales and reads him stories; if he is unlucky, she dumps him before the television or leaves him to the baby sitter. The mother has great responsibility for the development of his imagination and his taste; much afterward depends on what he heard in those early years. Nor should she feed him pap. Fifty years ago for the first twelve months and more babies were nurtured on nauseous slops; today their infant jaws may even first encounter ground steak at six weeks. Nor should their literary diet be pabulum; they soon pass the "huggy bunny" stage, and they flourish on good strong fantasy.

But maybe I am prejudiced in this matter. In very early years my Aunt Sarah read me Bible stories from a luridly illustrated little book called *Line Upon Line,* with graphic pictures of what happened to the rebellious Israelites, and the ravens bringing large chunks of cake to Elijah isolated in the desert, and the wicked little boys who mocked Elisha's bald head and were torn in pieces by two she-bears. My father too had a head as bald as Elisha's, but I never risked bear or slipper by untimely comment.

My mother read me tales from Joseph Jacobs' *English Fairy Tales.* Our favorites were Titty Mouse and Tatty Mouse (overwhelmed by a collapsing wall) and Nimmy Nimmy Not—of which Rumpelstiltskin is a feeble variant. Jacobs' classic is not sparing of horrors or of certain facts of life, as that some old gentlemen do not like small boys, like Mr. Miacca, who ate one for his supper every evening. Jacobs also gave us the story of Mr. Fox, who made love to rich girls, inveigled them to his house and there slew them for their jewelry. But the victim was warned; over the first door was inscribed BE BOLD, and over the second BE BOLD, but over the third BE NOT TOO BOLD; and if she was, and opened it, she stumbled on the festering remains of her predecessors. And Jack and the Beanstalk, and the giant who disliked Jack (for good reason) and cried out

Fee, fi, fo, fum!
I smell the blood of an Englishman!
Be he alive or be he dead,
I'll grind his bones to make me bread!

Or the tale of Burd Ellen, who ran round a church widershins and endured the most painful adventures before she was rescued by Childe Rowland. One should *never* go round a church, or anything else, widershins (which, for those who do not know the word, means counterclockwise, or against the natural way of the sun, which is contrary to all natural law). And there was the story of the Laidly Worm, a horrid reptile, till kissed on the mouth, when she reverted to a beautiful maiden; my subsequent experiments on garden worms and caterpillars were disappointingly negative.

I doubt whether Jacobs did much harm to the egos of his small readers. My infant terrors came rather from reality; it took me months to recover from a visit to the Zoo where I first looked upon the beasts which roam in the night, and might claw me with the same eager appetite as the lions their raw gobbets of horseflesh. Doubtless *English Fairy Tales* is now condemned by the child psychologists to whose censorship we must all submit, however strongly we resent other kinds of control to the freedom of the individual to seek his own damnation.

If it be true that the individual in his progress from the ovum to the Ph.D. passes through all the stages of evolution, then small children have just reached paleolithic level. If allowed to behave naturally, they are very bloody-minded; lurid fantasy is their proper mental diet. Television, however, is another matter; its horrors are visible and leave nothing to the imagination.

A certain father of my acquaintance used to amuse his brood (aged eight to four) with the puppet drama of Punch and Judy. The story of Mr. Punch showed how that old reprobate began by throwing his howling infant out of the window (and how many other sleepless fathers have had firmly to suppress the like desire). When Judy, his wife, protested, he hit her over the head and so became the victim of the law. Then in turn he slew the hangman and the policeman (symbolizing the triumph of the individual over social convention). As he progressed, he slaughtered a host of other victims, depending on the number of puppets in the set. Mr. Punch is thus a myth of uninhibited man.

There are several endings to the drama. In one version Punch lays all his victims on the platform, triumphs over them, and so to bed. In another, Punch's last fight is with the crocodile (or the Devil). After a terrific struggle, Punch is carried away to his proper reward; but, alternatively, he may slay the crocodile (or Devil), perhaps symbolizing thereby the final triumph of natural man over moral law.

This father usually chose the first ending; the parade and catalogue of the dead. Once, by way of a change he ended with the crocodile pulling Punch down to the depths. His children were dumb with astonished horror. Then they shouted at him with indignation: "Never, never do that again, Daddy; we won't have poor Mr. Punch eaten"—which was a fine corroboration of Bunyan's opinion that the young are naturally predestined for hell-fire. As it happens, those particular children grew up into model and very religious adults.

As soon as he can read, the child should be allowed to roam at will among books of all kinds, of which wise parents have a large store in the home, adult as well as juvenile; but parents should not attempt openly to supervise the reading of their child unless invited with "What shall I read next?" It is better to have many books available than to present a new book which the child is required to read. Children are naturally suspicious of such gifts. Tastes even among the very young differ greatly. Some love myths and fantasies; others are all for animal stories and nature; others for adventure and science; and even among the myth lovers there are favorites and rejects; those who are attracted by Odysseus are often bored by Odin.

Parents need great strength of character not to interfere or to prescribe. If the child picks up some hair-raising book (which father forgot to hide), there is no need for alarm; unless he is very precocious, the child usually finds it quite unreadable. He should be neither commanded nor even advised to abandon it as unedifying.

Above all, the Bible, which is basic to an understanding of European literature, needs delicate handling, for of all books it is the most important for readers of every age. But the young reader is handicapped by certain disadvantages. Most Bibles are still hideous specimens of bookmaking, printed in two columns of ugly type, chopped up into unnatural verses, bound in a solemn black imitation of leather. If the other books in the home are printed in comely type and well illustrated, the very look of the Sacred Scriptures repels. Children who are Protestant churchgoers hear portions read out every Sunday. The reader has a great responsibility. Bad—or, even worse, unctuous—reading ruins any child's enjoyment. Nor is the Bible undiluted suitable for the very young. Much of it—the Old Law, the Prophets and the sapiential books—is unintelligible; and though the famous stories are universal in the highest degree, some of the more infamous are better reserved for later reading. The parent who encourages his child to read the Bible entire must be prepared for shocks. I greatly embarrassed my mother by seeking light on the nature and significance of certain trophies which David took from the dead Philistines.

Before the cinema was fully established and long before radio and television, English boys were better provided with reading matter than today. For the very young there was a series of pink paperbacks, called *Books for Bairns,* at one penny a volume. The series included *The Ancient Mariner* and the story of Jason and the Golden Fleece, and other classical legends and myths. There were also "penny dreadfuls" (not encouraged by parents)—a whole saga of Dick Turpin, who in real life was a brutal highwayman, famous for his ride from London to York on his horse Black Bess. In the saga he was a romantic friend of the poor, everlastingly pursued by dishonest officers of the Law.

More reputable were the weeklies for boys, especially *The Boy's Own Paper,* regarded somewhat suspiciously by its readers, for the tone was high, and adventure was too often thickly sugared with uplift. Its rival, *Chums Annual,* came each Christmas in an enormous red volume of 800 pages and more; it took three months to read. *Chums* ran a serial, a blood-curdling yarn of pirates on the Spanish Main, written each year by one S. H. Walkley, luridly illustrated. There were also comic strips, and a host of short stories, miscellaneous articles on many matters, including celebrities of all kinds from professional footballers to prodigious infant musicians, as well as seemly quips and jokes. And there were great green volumes called *The World of Adventure,* full of true tales of battles and sea fights, famous and forgotten, of voyages of discovery, of Livingstone and Speke, of Red Indians, and Kelly the Australian bushranger, and Lord Ferrers, justly hanged for beating one of his servants to death, the first Englishman to perish by the drop, which was specially invented to break his aristocratic neck. From all these the young reader absorbed a mass of miscellaneous, unrelated but remembered facts.

Of all writers for boys, the most popular was G. A. Henty. Henty had been a war correspondent and he devised a most successful formula for historical tales. Each volume was concerned with some famous commander or event. The first chapter introduced the hero, aged eighteen—handsome, strong, heroic and British. The second chapter was straight history, and so on alternately until page 351, when the hero, after magnificent endeavors, for which he was highly honored by his emperor, king, general, or admiral (according to context), married the lovely heiress whom he had rescued in Chapter 16. Thereafter he passed rapidly to a ripe old age on page 352. Henty never let his readers down by lapsing into sex or sentimentality.

It was an excellent scheme, for a reader more intent on the story than the history could always skip the alternate chapters. Henty's gallant British boys (who had quite a remarkable family likeness) ranged all over time and place. Beric the Briton was one of the first. As a slave in Rome (where he was compulsorily trained as a gladiator) he rescued a Christian maiden from the very jaws of a lion. He rushed into the arena, equipped only with a cloak, which he skillfully tied over the head of the angry beast, and then subdued it to cringing by a smart kick on its blinded nose. Beric did, however, suffer a nasty gash on the thigh. This unexpected variation moved even the Emperor Nero to admiration and mercy. Nor did Henty confine himself to British wars. His boys served everywhere—with Frederick the Great, and even in Napoleon's disastrous Russian campaign, though England and France were then at war. But the hero, having been taken prisoner, was offered a chance of serving in the French Guard, an opportunity not to be missed. Thereafter he rose to the rank of sergeant and was awarded the Legion of Honor by the Emperor himself, who also bestowed a kiss on each blushing cheek.

I was one of Henty's greatest admirers; he gave me a taste for historical adventure. Scott I read all through one summer in the country when I was nine, and I even enjoyed him, as soon as I had developed the technique, which was to skip all the descriptions of scenery and the longer conversations and to read only for the story. *Ivanhoe* was my favorite, five times read at least. Years later I started to read it as a treat to my own children, but after a quarter of an hour we agreed to lay it aside; in the interval it had gone moldy. I did make renewed and conscientious efforts to appreciate Scott when I was stationed in Edinburgh in 1940, but he was artificially gothic as his monument, and as costive as the local diet of porridge and scones. There is a good thesis topic here: "Diet and literature—a psychosomatic study of the results of constipation on creative literary art."

In encouraging the young to read, the golden rule is therefore never to impose upon them. Every child's taste is different. Let each have ample opportunity to sample and reject for himself. Usually a child is bored by the inspiring classic which so enthralled his parents at his age; his sensitive spots are different. Herein lies also one of the great difficulties in prescribing class reading for teenagers (and younger). If they are made to read and study what once pleased their teachers, they find it tedious and develop a distaste for books which is permanently and irretrievably disastrous.

Unless reading is a natural and spontaneous joy, a student should avoid the study of English literature, which has become a vast undertaking, for the mass of writing that must be included within any definition of literature is so immense. Sixty years ago educated men shared a common stock of accepted literature: the Greek and Roman classics, the Bible, and a limited collection of English and European masterpieces. Contemporary works were in a different class; they had yet to prove their permanent worth. English literature as a subject for serious academic study was still suspect; the works even of Shakespeare and Milton were studied rather as philological and classical specimens than for delight.

The study of English literature, as a recognized academic discipline, is fairly recent in England. At Cambridge, the first tripos devoted to English was founded in 1917, and candidates for honors first sat for the examination in 1920. I was among them. Before the First World War, I had been a classic, but when I returned after four and a half years' service as a soldier, I revolted against the grammarians who dominated the Classical Tripos, and I sensed that English was likely to supplant

Latin and Greek as a training in the humanities. When I told my classical tutor, he snorted indignantly: "That novel-reading tripos! Quite worthless!" Hostility toward English literary studies persisted for at least two decades, and longer at the University of London, where the philologists were in great strength.

Nevertheless, there was much to be said for this attitude. Academic study was confined to works that had endured for at least two generations. Today, for better or worse, the distinction has been obliterated with the result that the criticism of current literature has passed to the academics, so that young writers, and especially poets, appeal for judgment no longer to the common reader but to the professors of criticism whose criteria are so special that any best seller is self-condemned, or at least suspect. Even when the professor descends to notice, it is no longer to enjoy the book for its own sake but to probe into its myths, symbols and archetypes.

Modern students of literature are thus offered such a vast menu of fare that the stock of reading shared by all readers in common is far smaller than it was sixty years ago. Today's common reader may have read more but he knows less than his grandfather. An allusion to the commonest of classical legends baffles him; even the Bible is an unknown book. Confront any batch of selected students (even graduates) of literature with Ham, Ahab (of Israel—not *Moby Dick*), Hezekiah, Lot's wife, or Elijah's ravens and they return a universal blank. However, they show greater response to Moses, Samson and Delilah, David and Bathsheba, whom Hollywood has exploited.

IV. SCHOLARSHIP

While the intelligent student of literature finds delight in any piece of memorable writing, his pleasure can be increased by enlightenments provided by the professional guides. These are of two kinds: scholars and critics. They are not, or should not be, rivals, for a critic must be something of a scholar, and a scholar with no critical sense is just a pedant. Each, however, has different functions. The main business of the scholar is to give the reader such information as he needs about the text of a work of literature, the exact meaning of words, the background of the matter. It is for the critic to interpret wider significance, to demonstrate literary techniques, to explain the ideas and to relate them to the larger body of general knowledge. The nearer a book comes to the life, environment and experience of the reader, the less need for scholars and critics to interpose their comments. There is another function which scholars and critics share: the general picture of English literature as a whole, the writing of literary history.

Scholarship is another form of pleasure, though rarer and more specialized than good reading. Like the skin diver who brings up treasures from an old wreck, the scholar has his excitements as he wrestles with Oblivion and recovers from the dead past the facts of history or biography, or traces the workings of a mind long since silent, or even establishes the correct reading of a text. Scholarship brings its own rewards, known only to those who have practiced the art; but it is not an activity for the common reader, though he often benefits from the labors of scholars, who alone can restore freshness to an ancient work of art. The pleasures of scholarship begin where the pleasures of literature end.

One of the first tasks of the scholar is to establish the text, that is, to give the reader the actual words written by the author. With modern works, where the author corrects his own proofs at leisure and is aided by copy editors and proofreaders, there should seldom be much difficulty about the text; yet it is a common experience of all authors that the most regrettable misprint can escape half a dozen proofreadings and pass through several editions before some eager reader denounces it. Examples of this shame need not here be particularized.

The more ancient the text, the greater the likelihood of error. Sixteenth- and seventeenth-century texts, especially of plays and poems, are often corrupt. Sometimes different versions survive of the same poem. There are four versions of Herrick's "Farewell unto Poetry," each with some variant readings. Sometimes, as with *Hamlet,* there are two good versions and one bad, each adding or omitting significant passages. Further back, in the days before printing, the difficulties are even greater, as the labors of Manly and Rickert on the text of Chaucer have amply shown. Sometimes an author himself revised or enlarged his original version, as happened with Wordsworth's *Prelude* and Bunyan's *Grace Abounding.* It is for the scholar to unravel these tangles.

Textual problems concern the scholarly editor, to whose labors every reader is indebted. But the editing of a text is complex and soon leads the editor far away from its content. He passes from the author to the printed book, and thence back to the printer and his types and formes and methods, to the printing trade and its organization, to booksellers and their shops, with passing observations on watermarks, worm holes and the chemical analysis of ink.

That subdivision of scholarship miscalled bibliography—meaning the study of all that goes to the physical making of a book—is a vast study, but it is not literary study, and for students of literature its results sometimes seem hardly worth while. The textualists have indeed settled (at least to their own satisfaction) a few disputed texts and readings, and have left others more disputable than ever. "The dram of eale" is still a doubt, and no one yet knows (in spite of Fredson Bowers) whether Hamlet's flesh was "too too solid," or "sullied," or "sallied"; nor indeed would an auditor in the Globe have been better informed, for all three words were pronounced "sarlid."

"Bibliography" is not to be belittled. It is the most fascinating study, detective work on real problems, which calls for minute inquiry and ingenious deduction. It also has the certain advantages for the bibliographer. No one can dispute his findings until he has himself made the same minute examination of the text; and since a refutation requires at least three times the length of the original statement, few journals would publish it. Bibliography is not literary study, but the study of how a book was manufactured; its light on literature is incidental and occasional.

A more important concern of the scholar is to elucidate the meaning of the words used by the author. Words are constantly changing their meanings and associations. At first reading of any book more than a hundred years old we meet this difficulty. Thus, for instance, the words "secure," "security." Once "secure" meant "without a care"—*se cura*. "Upon my secure hour thine uncle crept"—the unbuttoning time when a man took his nap of an afternoon. And from that, "security" degenerates to "foolhardy carelessness," especially in looking after the morals of one's wife. Thence it ascended to "wise watchfulness" and a "sense of safety"; and so to today's meaning of "elaborate precautions to safeguard military secrets." When Bacon wrote of "science" and "art," he meant pure and applied knowledge, and in his day the scientist was called a philosopher, a title which most modern scientists would repudiate with horror. Shakespeare's plays abound in words which have radically changed their meanings, or—more difficult to appreciate—their subtler connotations. A glance at the footnotes usually sets us right, but there is far more to this constant change than immediate and direct meaning.

Words take their meanings from their contexts and their times, so that a reader cannot appreciate the full meaning without a knowledge of a word's environment. To re-create the visual image evoked by the phrase "the portrait of a beautiful lady," the reader must know, if not the name of the artist, at least the period of its painting. With this knowledge he can visualize style and costume. Even if the lady has no costume, his imagination needs to know whether the picture was painted by Botticelli or by Reubens, by Gauguin or Matisse, or by one of the very moderns. In reading "The Lady of Shalott" he must realize that the equipment used by the reapers reaping early was provided by the local blacksmith and not by International Harvester.

When it comes to those phrases which express ideas, a discerning reader must know something at least of ideas generally current when the book was written. Much modern scholarly study of an author is devoted to his ideas and his intellectual background. A critic who is ignorant of these matters goes far astray if he attempts to interpret a work of literature, or even its verbal imagery. To understand *Paradise Lost* he needs familiarity not only with the Bible but also with Homer, Virgil, the Greek tragedians, Ovid and Dante, Christian theology, and a host of current ideas of the physical universe, and (not least) the Latin tongue. The present decline in Milton's popularity arises largely because the younger critics lack this knowledge and are therefore incapable of understanding even the surface meaning of the poem.

Nor need we go to a poem so essentially literary as *Paradise Lost*. Even the simplest line in Shakespeare will often fail to evoke its full meaning without the aid of a scholar. In *A Midsummer Night's Dream* it is said of the Fairy Queen that "the cowslips tall her pensioners be"—one of several lines wherein Shakespeare, in creating Fairyland, tries to make us realize that fairies are quite tiny: elves can creep into acorn cups, fairies make themselves coats of bats' wings, and as for the Fairy Queen herself—"the cowslips tall her pensioners be." To understand the line we need to visualize both cowslips and pensioners.

The English cowslip is a wild flower. It appears in the pasture fields late in April before the meadow grass has grown and it stands up straight and conspicuous with a stalk about nine inches high, crowned with a drooping cluster of golden freckled bell-like flowerets. The word "pensioner" suggests to most American readers an aged employee, pensioned off and in retirement; it calls up corncob pipes and a rocking chair on the porch. But that was not Shakespeare's meaning. In his time the Gentlemen Pensioners of Queen Elizabeth's bodyguard were a small *corps d'élite* of young men of the best families who lived in the palace and were directly responsible for guarding the Queen's person. They were chosen for their looks, their height and their physique; they were dressed resplendently and they carried gilt halberds—magnificent creatures. If therefore the Fairy Queen's tallest subjects were not more than cowslip high, inhabitants of Fairyland must be quite small. There is thus a world of meaning even in this one simple line; and the reader misses it if he lacks knowledge of the common objects of the English countryside and some antiquarian knowledge of the Elizabethan court. The line is pleasing enough in itself, but it means so much more to the reader who knows.

Another function of the scholar is to illumine the life and environment of the author. Much energy has been spent in unearthing the facts of biography, and more is often misspent in interpreting his words by that uncertain light, especially when the biographical records are scanty. The "biographical approach" is not always as valuable as it seems, the truth being that the more universal a work, the less important is it to know about its creator. Many objective facts have been discovered about Shakespeare, few of any intimate significance; but *Lear* would not have been a greater or a lesser work, more or less pleasurable, had its author been anonymous. The facts unearthed about Marlowe show a blasphemer and an atheist; life and plays taken together reveal clues to the psychology of Marlowe himself; but Marlowe's psychology concerns psychologists, not students of literature.

Nevertheless there are two ways of regarding a work of literary art—as an experience complete in itself and isolated from its creator, or as documentary evidence for the study of the author's psyche. Many critics who are amateur psychologists and psychologists who are amateur critics have so regarded literature, not always with convincing success. Freud himself was convinced that Shakespeare's works were written by Edward de Vere, Earl of Oxford; which may by some be regarded as strong evidence for Oxford; and by others that Freud's critical abilities were rudimentary. Few common readers agree with the she-psychiatrist who found clear evidence in Lear's ravings that Shakespeare as a child suffered such infantile rage during a pregnancy of his mother that he befouled his little pants; though Ernest Jones' psychoanalytic *Hamlet and Oedipus* has found many readers, some wonder whether the real complex lurked in the subconscious of Hamlet, of Shakespeare, or of Ernest Jones.

On the other hand an understanding of Donne is enhanced by a knowledge of his life, for his poetry is an expression of his struggles, frustrations and adventures, physical, emotional and spiritual. The more known about Donne the man, the more meaningful his poetry; but to understand his poems and his images and patterns of thought, a reader needs a vast knowledge of sixteenth- and seventeenth-century social history, theology, psychology, science and literary lore. Far more needs to be known before the poetry can be fully understood; yet that understanding will take the reader (who will have long ceased to be a common reader) far far away from literary pleasure.

Sometimes the facts of biography seriously mar enjoyment of a work because the personality of the author intrudes. The little we know of Milton's family life is too much; and though the resurrection of Annette Vallon has humanized William Wordsworth, there are bitter regrets that Leslie Hotson ever unearthed Shelley's letters to Harriet; it is difficult to accept as a self-appointed guide to human conduct a man who was so crassly ignorant of human nature. Universal literature has no need of these details, but they illuminate the less universal. Some authors, indeed, cannot be understood until the reader has first inspected the washing hanging on the line.

A further activity of the scholar, and perhaps the most important, is true research: the discovery of facts and records hitherto unknown. In the present century many such discoveries have been made that throw new light on the life and personality of authors, of which some of the most romantic and sensational are recorded in Richard Altick's *The Scholar Adventures.* But the graduate student should not be misled into forgetting that scholarship involves far more days of sheer drudgery than moments of exciting discovery.

Literary scholarship is not so much a direct contribution to literature as the pursuit of the truth about literary men and matters. The scholar himself needs an acute and perceptive mind and a keen sense to evaluate and set forth his facts, as well as an appreciation of what the common reader may need. The test of a great work of scholarship is that it answers all the questions that any reader may reasonably ask; such are E. K. Chambers' volumes on Elizabethan Stage and the facts and problems of Shakespearean scholarship; R. B. McKerrow's edition of *The Works of Thomas Nashe,* W. W. Greg's edition of *Henslowe's Diary* and *Papers,* his bibliography of Elizabethan Drama, and his study of the First Folio; Percy Simpson's edition of Ben Jonson's works; James Spedding's Life of Francis Bacon. Of another kind, John Livingstone Lowes' *The Road to Xanadu* is also great scholarship; it is not so much a contribution to the appreciation or understanding of *The Ancient Mariner* or *Kubla Khan* as a demonstration of the strange ways in which Coleridge's mind worked.

V. CRITICISM

Of critics, the reviewer is the lowest form of life, but (like the earthworm) necessary, for so many books are published week by week that some hand sorting and selection is essential.

Reviews are of various kinds and degrees. Those printed in

daily or weekly journals are usually written in haste to report the birth of new books; and every reputable journal keeps its crew of reviewers, some of whom are themselves authors. Although three in five young students of literature (especially women) yearn to become reviewers, the trade is dismal, for the reviewer must read not for delight but for dollars. Yet book reviewers can usually choose their own hours of work; a dramatic critic must deliver his judgments by midnight before going to bed. Few fates can be worse than to be forced each week to read a dozen books or to watch three or more new plays. A professional reviewer's digestion is soon ruined, and like other dyspeptics he suffers a perpetual peevishness which he vents on the causes of his distress. Besides, as a matter of original sin, he may soon learn to take a devilish delight in showing his own superior wit at the expense of a victim who can seldom hit back; he may also develop a dictator complex, especially if his own efforts at authorship have been second-rate.

The great days of the reviewer-dictator are now past, and few moderns, except for an occasional historian, dare pronounce judgments so haughty and superior as the Scottish reviewers who tormented Keats and his contemporaries. Macaulay was the greatest of the tribe; lesser men in later generations affected the same universal ability, of whom in England Edmund Gosse was perhaps the last. The present-day reviewer who weekly contributes his signed article to the book columns of the Sunday paper is usually more careful to affect a geniality, or at least a modesty, which forestalls rough retaliation; for most reviewers realize that although an author must perforce submit to their rulings, yet the reviewer in turn will be judged by the author and his friends. The literary reputation of a reviewer can be marred as well as made by his review. This consolation is denied to those appraised in the *Times Literary Supplement,* which still keeps up the principle of anonymity to preserve a kind of faceless omniscience. An author who suffers from a harsh review is thus left uncertain whether his masked judge is an expert, an envious rival, or just Johannes Factotum (ex-Oxford don).

Reviews in the learned journals are more deliberately composed but of less use, for they seldom appear until the book has been published for at least a year; and by that time all who are interested in the subject have long since made their own judgments. Most learned reviews are little more than obituary notices of a book.

However, a young author need not be unduly depressed by a harsh judgment; reviews make little difference to the sale or the popularity of a book. In my own experience those books which have been most successful have received little notice from reviewers; and those which have been most kindly praised have sold least. One publisher said to me bitterly that he had small use for reviews and regarded an enthusiastic notice as a kiss of death! This attitude, however, is not universal; other publishers of my acquaintance are hypersensitive to reviews and regard them as all-important.

The true end of a review is not to enhance the reputation of the reviewer but to tell the inquiring reader whether he should buy or read this book among so many. Surely much space could be saved in the popular papers if some kind of formula were to be devised, on the lines of the ratings of films given by the Consumers Union or the Legion of Decency. A new novel could then be reviewed in a truly scientific and objective manner. It would be submitted to a large panel of readers of varied tastes, each of whom would mark squares in a card; and the results would be tabulated and averaged. Appropriate abbreviations could be devised. Thus: C = Crime; W = Western; A = Adultery, etc. One to three stars would denote excellence in the class. *Lady Chatterley's Lover* would receive the highest rating of A***, which should satisfy everyone. By using such a formula quite full book reviews could be printed in a single line of type.

On a higher level, critics, who are not merely concerned with last week's new books but with all literature, can be divided into three kinds: *tasters, enthusiasts* and *analysts.*

Tasters are those who express opinions about literature based on personal intuition. They reject formal rules, for they believe that experienced and intelligent readers have a sort of common feeling for the best. They are in the same class as tasters of wine, tea or cigars, whose judgments are respected because general experience shows them to be just. The taster critics have read widely, enjoy literature and they try to justify their preferences. This kind of criticism was more popular in the past than today; its bulk is enormous. One of its greatest practitioners was George Saintsbury, who had omnivorous experience of all European literature and who expressed his likes and dislikes with gusto. He was also an expert judge of wine.

Tasters at their best enhance enjoyment by a kind of infectious zest, showing all kinds of subtleties and delights overlooked by the common reader, whose own critical taste is thereby made more acute. They aim at creating works of art inspired by works of art. But they seldom encourage new experiments or unfamiliar ways of expression, and their judgments are often rejected or ignored by later generations. In the famous year 1798 they welcomed Thomas Campbell's *The Pleasures of Hope* as a great poem; they rejected the *Lyrical Ballads* as puerile. In the 1910's they regarded William Watson, Henry Newbolt and Alfred Noyes as the most promising of modern poets. Criticism of this kind instinctively reflects the literary fashions of the moment. Its colors soon fade; but while fresh it is enjoyable reading for we are in the company of good talkers who share our own tastes.

Enthusiasts are tasters who are moved to a kind of ecstasy by the literary and other arts, which they eulogize rhapsodically. Swinburne and Ruskin were good examples; and of modern writers G. Wilson Knight at his best on some of Shakespeare's plays. Enthusiasm, however, can very soon degenerate into gush, when it becomes ridiculous.

The *analysts,* as a race of critics, have flourished particularly in the past forty years. They are of two kinds. Some are mainly concerned with the general analysis of the literary art, and particularly of poetry; Aristotle was the original founder of the sect. Others examine minutely individual poems.

This analytic kind of criticism is in theory semiscientific. It borrows largely from psychology and it has created a formidable vocabulary of technical terms. It is sometimes called the New Criticism. At its best it is a reaction against undisciplined enthusiasm and the frivolity of some of the older kinds of scholarship; it brings us back to the work of art itself and reveals many hitherto unsuspected depths in the human mind. Its disadvantages are considerable. The New Criticism is expounded in appalling professional jargon so that reading becomes a science for experts, who are concerned with ontologies, spatial forms, objective correlatives, meaning-relationships, internal references, repetitive form, syllogistic and qualitative progressions.

Not everyone admires the New Criticism, but so long as it is recognized for what it is—a fashion of contemporary opinion on literary matters—it has its importance. The new critics are no more infallible than the old, but even less endowed with humility. "The sole purpose of criticism," says one of them, "is to enlighten the reader, to instruct the reader, to create the proper reader" . . . presumably one like themselves. Unfortunately the new critics seldom laugh, and never at themselves.

In the early days of Christianity when the faith began to affect intellectuals, there arose a form of heresy known as Gnosticism. The Gnostics were men in the know, rare minds who withdrew from the common herd. Not for them the crudities of the four canonical gospels or your common vulgar Christian. They were the enlightened ones; they devised their own obscure vocabulary and they invented a mythology in which to express their superior knowledge; they also rewrote their own gospels. They were a great danger to the Christian faith, and the Holy Church condemned them wholeheartedly. They must have been intolerable bores. There is a considerable element of neo-gnosticism in today's neo-criticism.

In truth, there is a current confusion about literary study. More than eighty pages of notes and bibliography in René Wellek and Austin Warren's *Theory of Literature* record a mass and variety of literary "approaches." A closer and dispassionate look reveals that of all these literary studies, very few are studies *of* literature; most of them are, rather, studies arising *out of* literature—a very different matter. We can make an analogy, not wholly frivolous. In the United States 80,000,000 turkeys are bred annually for two purposes: to provide the farmer with an income and the citizen with a feast. The study of turkeys would be concerned with two relevant topics only: the breeding, hatching, rearing and marketing of turkeys, and the buying, preparing, cooking and eating of turkeys. Nevertheless learned gallopavists may take great delight in discussing such problems as the pigmentation of wattles, the spatial forms of tail feathers, the psychological reactions of frustrated hens, or the semantic, imagist, symbolic or archetypal aspects of gobbledygook. Yet interesting as these aspects may be to the specialist, they have no relevance to Thanksgiving dinners. Similarly most of the studies enumerated by Wellek and Warren are irrelevant to the study of literature.

In this very profusion of literary studies and specializations threatens an impending disaster. If the common reader, on approaching the door marked ENGLISH LITERATURE, finds himself confronted with a large notice—KEEP OUT. HIEROPHANTS ONLY—he will silently tiptoe away and leave literature to the *littérateurs.* There is a great danger that the study of English literature may be destroyed by the new critics as the study of the classics was destroyed by the old grammarians.

The true study of literature is concerned with that which adds to the delight of the reader. It follows that the teacher of English must first enjoy reading and then be able to convey his own delight to his students.

2 ✦ *Fantastic Interlude: English at the University of New Atlantis*

It so happened that while I was writing the previous chapter I was also offering a course entitled "Great Writers of the English Renaissance," among them Francis Bacon. Not the least memorable of his works is that unfinished fantasy called *New Atlantis,* his dream of the scientists' Utopia. Bacon's dream has been fulfilled. In any great modern university there is a ceaseless pursuit of research into natural phenomena, into "the knowledge of Causes and secret motions of things; and the enlarging of the bounds of Human Empire, to the effecting of all things possible."

Yet Bacon would have recognized the dangers of all this activity. In *The Advancement of Learning* he had already warned against the extreme affecting of two extremities, "the one Antiquity, the other Novelty; wherein it seemeth the children of Time do take after the nature and malice of the father. For as he devoureth his children, so one of them seeketh to devour and suppress the other; while antiquity envieth there should be new additions, and novelty cannot be content to add but it must deface."

Another error, he wrote, is "that after the distribution of particular arts and sciences, men have abandoned universality, or *philosophia prima;* which cannot but cease and stop all progression." And yet another error is "that men have used to infect their meditations, opinions, and doctrines, with some conceits which they have most admired, or some sciences which they have most applied; and given all things else a tincture according to them, utterly untrue and unproper."

Had Bacon lived today, the modern Father of Solomon's House would have given a very different account of its activities after three centuries and more of intense scientific research into the "secret motions of things." It would have run to this effect:

"You shall understand," said the Father of the English House, "that at the time when your Francis Bacon visited the Island of New Atlantis we were far advanced in our studies of the causes and nature of things, following the tradition of the Founder of our commonweal, who was no less than the wise King Solomon, whose wisdom excelled the wisdom of all the children of the East country. He spake three thousand proverbs, and his songs were a thousand and five; and he spake of trees from the cedar tree that is in Lebanon even unto the hyssop that springeth out of the wall: he spake of beasts, and of fowl, and of creeping things and of fishes. Taught by this example we hold that for a man of learning, or for a teacher, the greatest of gifts is universal curiosity. His eyes see everything; his ears are always open; he has a mind that receives, absorbs, and compares all impressions.

"In former times, while most of our learned men applied themselves each to his special science, others were employed in surveying the whole of knowledge at home and abroad whom we called by such names as Merchants of Light or Dowry-men or Benefactors. For some generations the study of the several sciences was pursued with ever-increasing exactitude until so much knowledge had been heaped together that every science needed its own language, and no one, not even the Merchants of Light, could any longer understand what his fellow was saying. Moreover, it was manifest that in pursuing the causes of Things, we were neglecting the study of the essence of Man. For this cause we began to enlarge our university and to erect new houses for the study of the humane learning, as the History House, the Greek House, the French House and the rest. Of the new houses, the English House is the greatest, since English has become the common tongue of our Island.

"At the time of the foundation of our English House there was much debate concerning its ends, for it is our firmest tradition that the first plot or plan of any new enterprise shall be to determine its final end or purpose. When that has been agreed, then we consider the best means of achieving it. The aim or end of our English House is to achieve that kind of universal knowledge of humanity which so distinguished our wise Founder. This is the most important of all knowledge, and to this end all our learned men, whatever their particular science, must spend some time in the House of English so that they may learn to understand each other. Our House of English is thus the most respected, as it is the greatest of all.

"We have included within the House certain smaller schools, as of Grammar and Linguistic, where the mysteries of languages are expertly examined, but in our general teaching we make no fine distinction between studies of language and studies of literature, for a man cannot understand literature unless first he be expert in language, nor can he be expert in language until he can understand literature. Naturally we teach the structure of the language and we are careful to demand that words always be used with an exact sense of their meaning; but our students are so trained in their early years that they use the language instinctively; as a baby after it has learned to walk needs no formal lessons, though it may need occasional exercises to improve its movements.

"The first teaching of literature begins in earliest days. As soon as a child can talk, it is encouraged to listen to stories. These are carefully chosen both for the content, and for their language; it is most important that the child always hear good speech. Tellers of stories for the young are held in high honor among us. Many of the tales are traditional; they came into the language from the Greek, the Latin, and also from the sacred Hebrew writings. Some children are themselves natural storytellers and have a kind of visionary gift. We take special note of such, for they are the creative artists of the next generation; just as other children have a natural gift for using their hands and for puzzles; these will be our scientists. Both kinds are selected for appropriate training as soon as they are ready, for in our first elementary education we are careful to separate children according to their gifts; our aim is not uniformity but diversity. That training which best suits the child of a practical mind ruins the visionary. We never force a child prematurely. A visionary child loses his power of vision if he is forced to read before he is ready. This visionary gift we regard as most precious; it can too easily be destroyed.

"We do not (as in some countries) submit our children to any kind of formal or (as they call it) 'objective' tests; instead we observe them, for we regard our experienced observers as less fallible guides than some mechanical device or statistic. From the first we are all trained to observe. For the very young, we have games of the kind described by the English writer Kipling in his book *Kim*. A child is told to shut his eyes and to describe everything about him; or he is asked to describe a picture, or the whole progress of some team game. Thus observation becomes a habit and instinctive. At the same time we train the memory, and for that we have other exercises. When he has heard a story, the child repeats it, word for word. Every schoolboy learns certain passages by rote daily.

Others who have an aptitude for drawing are encouraged to draw what they have seen either with their eyes or in their imaginations.

"In later life observation and memory have become habits. Our good students of literature have memories so large and accurate that they can repeat most famous poems without book. Nor do we allow students to take notes of what they hear: they remember.

"As for instruction in reading, in this we find little difficulty. Most children are eager to learn. Good readers are highly regarded; and bad readers are mocked. We do not allow silent reading in the early stages. Children love to hear their own voices, and in this way they develop a natural eagerness for the sounds of words and rhythms. When they have become serious readers—about the twelfth year—they play a game called 'Quotations.' Two or more will carry on a conversation entirely in quotations from what they have read. It can be very entertaining when the contestants have keen wits; we regard it as a civilized amusement. Certainly it needs good memory, but good memory is the first quality needed by a scholar or a teacher, so long as it is combined with an alert mind.

"When boys and girls leave school at the age of seventeen they enter the *Gymnasion* or college and now they begin the serious study of literature. They are given lists of the best books and a short history; and thereafter they wander at will among the books in the Library, though most of them are eager to posses their own books which they can obtain very cheaply, for the State subsidizes the printing of good books. In the *Gymnasion* our manner of teaching is to gather these young students into groups of twelve, called Fellowships. They meet once a week for two hours with their professor, who asks them about the books which each has read and what each student found in his reading; at these meetings also one or more of them reads an essay or other piece of writing to his fellows. There is little need for further instruction. All can read intelligently, and write, or they would not have been admitted to the *Gymnasion*.

"There are also certain public exercises such as debates and discourses. In debates two students defend a position which two others attack; and in the discourses one student delivers a speech or lecture without notes on some topic before his fellows or even before the whole *Gymnasion*. The professors also debate in this manner and offer discourses once a month as models for their students. This method is founded upon the old academic discipline of the fifteenth and sixteenth centuries which produced such notable writers and poets.

"Nor do we hold examinations or tests. At the end of every month, each of the students and the professor in a Fellowship is given twelve cards—two white (to denote the best), five red, three blue and two green (for the weakest). Students and professor secretly inscribe each card with one name, but without further comment. At the end of the year the two students in each Fellowship who win most white cards are awarded a white ribbon, and so with the other colors. Occasionally a student wins all white cards; he is distinguished by a gold ribbon. We have no other tests, for we find by experience that our students are good judges of each other. In each year from those who have won gold or white ribbons we choose a score to be prepared as Apprentices for the English House. They have already studied literature (which includes writing, reading and public speaking) for three years. They now receive four years of special preparation.

"In their first year they learn about Life. Since literature is largely concerned with the common experiences of life, we send them to live near the earth for four seasons. They dig, plow, ride horses, milk cows, mend hedges and the like; and they are given also some experience of the sea. These lessons they learn by living with farmers of the smaller kind who work their own farms, and for a while also with fishermen. Such men though they have small aptitude for books have much natural lore and practical wisdom. Moreover, we hold it good for students (whose heads at this age are overfull of book learning) to understand that many men regard their studies as unnecessary and frivolous. They learn also about the natural phenomena—the stars and the winds, the phases of the moon (so seldom even seen by city dwellers), the procession of the seasons, the journeyings of birds and the like. This kind of education is given to all students in the Houses of the Humanities.

"Nevertheless apprentices in the first year are not deprived of reading. They read books suitable to their environment. Moreover they themselves report on their own progress. Each is required daily to record what he has done and observed in a journal which is sent each month to the Rector of the House. It gives a clear insight into the apprentice's power of observation and of expression, and also of his character.

"The second year is the English Year. We now send our apprentices to England, where they live for periods of several successive weeks in different environments, with selected families for the most part, but for some of the time in colleges and universities. It is a profitable privilege for the family, for a high fee is paid. The host is required to instruct his student in English ways. Again, at the end of each period, the apprentice sends in his journal from which we see what he has learned and how faithfully the host has fulfilled his obligation.

"During this year the apprentice is required to observe particularly certain aspects of English life, such as their pageantry and ceremonial, which particularly interests us, for in New Atlantis (as you will know from Bacon's description) we are exact and elaborate in our ritual observances. We regard ritual, scrupulously performed, as a most civilizing influence.

"I myself," declared the Father, "when I was an apprentice in England was fortunate to be a witness of their most elaborate ceremony—the Coronation of a Sovereign, which is most intricately ordered and full of symbols so ancient that few are now understood. Everyone has his place, rank and particular duty; and each wears a striking and colorful costume.

"But they observe similar ceremonies on many occasions. In the universities, the doctors wear peculiar hats and gowns of scarlet silk lined with the different colors of their faculties. In their law courts, judges and barristers who plead before them not only wear gowns but wigs of the kind once fashionable in the eighteenth century, very hot indeed and inconvenient; but this ritual adornment together with elaborate procedures makes the process of the law terrifying to the common citizen. Even their schoolmasters wear academic gowns when teaching a class. Thus in every walk of life there is a kind of hierarchy of place, outwardly symbolized. Such a universal system cannot but instill certain instincts.

"Also," he said, "I was set to study the code of the English Gentleman, which I found very intricate, for so few agreed in the definition of this word 'gentleman.' I read widely in books ancient and modern, and I asked many whom I met to enlighten me. They were reluctant to reply, for while everyone seemed to know the answer, they could not put it into words. One said, 'One of us.' Another, whom I found boorish and illiterate, answered me rudely, 'What I am and you are not.' This man was possessed of a title and was member of three exclusive clubs; he was very rich, the family honors and wealth having descended to him from his grandfather, who made a great fortune by dealing in junk during one of the wars.

"In England so many things are a matter of feeling, of intuition, never of definition. A gentleman has certain attitudes, and a language within a language. No gentleman will use certain phrases. It is not a question of profanity or obscenity; I have heard the foulest obscenity and profanity (albeit very witty) from one who by any count was a perfect gentleman. Nor does the gentleman's code necessarily imply a moral standard; the rate of divorce and adultery is higher among the gentlemen than the average of the population.

"There is a considerable literature on this subject, but all the writers seem to be confused. Most of them grudgingly admit that a gentleman needs to be a man with money. The first Lord Burleigh, Queen Elizabeth I's great minister, declared that gentility was but ancient riches; in his case a matter of only three generations, for the family was quite humble in origin. It is not, however, merely money but, rather, that money admits a man into the circles where the secret code is understood and practiced. Two or more generations ago the social barrier between gentlemen and the rest was more definitely marked. No gentleman would accept hospitality from one whom he regarded as his social inferior—his tailor, for example, or his grocer.

"An officer in the Army or Navy was by virtue of his rank and position a gentleman, no matter what his origin; and it is perhaps in the officers' code that we can best sense the distinctions. An officer can get drunk discreetly. He can seduce his brother officer's wife, but not the wife of his sergeant. He can neglect his duties; but if he presents a worthless check, or fails to honor his gambling debts, then he is cast out of the order. Every gentleman will instinctively do certain things; and no gentleman will do certain other things; but these things are never codified. In this, as in so many of the customs of the race, the distinctions are very real but quite indefinable; they can only be perceived by feeling. I found all this a most valuable lesson in the understanding of English literature and especially in my later studies of the eighteenth and nineteenth centuries, where the distinctions were more significant than today. But I digress.

"The third is the Creative Year. The apprentices now return to the English House and spend their time in creating that which they will teach. They write stories, novels, dramas, poems. Moreover they act in plays and direct their performance. These efforts are fiercely criticized both by students and by professors. We regard it as essential for an apprentice to have had this experience of writing so that he may know at first hand the writer's problems and difficulties. In any activity the instructor must himself be able to practice the art which he professes. There can be no confidence in a swimming instructor who cannot swim; nor do students have respect for a teacher of literature until he has shown that he can write. Nor is critical writing about literature enough, for much of it is ill-informed and therefore misleading, because the critic has never experienced in practice the mental processes of the writer whom he is criticizing. We have small use for such critics, and even less for those who lack grace of style and expression.

"The fourth is the Year of Application. In this final year the apprentice displays his acquired talents. He publicly demonstrates that he can read aloud with sympathy, fluency and intelligence. He is required to direct a Fellowship of students in the presence of their professor; and for these displays, the most critical and lively students are chosen. Once more he returns to debate and discourse; and finally he has to reveal his ability as a scholar by writing a short thesis on some topic, chosen for him by the Doctors of the House, which requires research, industry, accuracy, meditation and personality. When the thesis has been completed, it is read by a body of students and doctors, and the apprentice is closely questioned on his facts and their presentation. In some ways this inquisition resembles the oral examination for the degree of doctor of philosophy in American universities, but with important differences. Our interest is rather in the man and how he has revealed his mind and his abilities than in what he has written, which is of less importance. When the last question has been answered and the judges have accepted the thesis as a worthy piece of work, all copies are gathered together into a sack and solemnly burned in an ornamental brazier specially made for that purpose.

"Burning is the proper end of such exercises. There is an aptness in the flame and smoke which symbolizes the heat of achievement, the light of hope and the vanity of human endeavor. Besides, a young apprentice at the end of his four years is seldom able to produce mature work. If the topic has been rewarding, then it can be used again by others. Moreover, if we kept every thesis, in a short time there would be vast accumulation of theses which must be read by any luckless inquirer who wishes to pursue the like topic. Mere accumulation of books is no advantage; it clogs scholarship and deadens originality.

"Finally there is a concluding ceremony. All the successful apprentices are feasted by the Rector and the Fathers of the House, and as a climax of the evening the Rector hangs round the neck of each a silver chain bearing a medal inscribed with the head of King Solomon, our wise Founder. He also receives a small bronze box surmounted with a phoenix and containing the ashes of his thesis. By these symbolic acts the young men are welcomed among us as Masters of the English House.

"Thereafter five kinds of activity are expected of the Masters. They become Creators, Researchers, Compilers, Commentators and Teachers. Each has already in some measure experienced these activities; now each is encouraged to pursue that which most attracts him. Yet all have an obligation to the House. The Teachers must spend one third of their time in one of the other activities; and the others one third in teaching. A good teacher must always be learning, and a learned man must teach lest he become too cloistered from the world. None is regarded more highly than the others. All are encouraged to produce as each has been given his gift, but we are rigorous in scrutinizing written works; nor do we permit publication unless the work is regarded as new or important.

"Every work submitted for publication is read and judged by a Council of Nine, of whom three are young Masters who have not yet passed their fifth year in the House, three are Fathers, and three are in the middle rank of Doctors. In this way the natural conservatism of the elderly is balanced against the novelty-mongering of the young. The Council decides whether the work is to be rejected, or permitted to circulate for ten years in typescript, or to be published for twenty-five years. We do this because we believe that the number of books in the library of our English House and in circulation should remain constant at about 10,000 volumes. Every year certain of the Commentators are appointed to scrutinize the books which have reached the alloted limit. If a book has not been superseded and still shows vitality, it can be replaced in the shelves for another ten years when it will again be examined. However, outdated books are not destroyed; they are transferred to another building called the Mausoleum to which only Researchers and Compilers are admitted.

"Such in outline," concluded the Father, "are some of the customs in our English House in New Atlantis which seem most to differ from yours."

After this pleasant dream I came back to things as they are, not in New Atlantis but in Lower Michigan and elsewhere. I descended to my sophomores of English 68, nominally concerned with Masterpieces of English Literature, and quaintly categorized in the announcement as a "recitation course," which means little serious reading and much immature talk. I probed gently into their early training in myth, story and legend, regarded as so important in New Atlantis. Results were negative. No one had heard of Jepthah's daughter, or Atalanta's apple, or could throw light on that memorable occasion when Joshua bade the sun stand still—an event which in later years caused such mortification to Galileo Galilei. The foundations on which to build an appreciation of English literature were woefully sandy. I abandoned fantasy to face reality.

3 ✦ *As Things Are*

University teachers of English, especially in America, suffer because the first of the principles in New Atlantis is so seldom observed; nowhere is there any statement or definition of the agreed purpose of their teaching or indeed of their existence. Moreover, universities are of different kinds and pursue different aims. Once there was a time (perhaps only in the era of Once-upon-a-time) when a university was an association of learned men, banded together to pursue knowledge for its own sake. In such an institution teaching was a subsidiary, and not always even a necessary, activity. Yet teaching had its uses. Even profound scholars need an audience (however limited) to whom they may disclose their achievements, and apprentices who will ultimately succeed them. That kind of institution still exists in a few places, and in a few departments in some others where scholars are supported to follow learning which has no immediate, or even remote, material advantage: such, for instance, as the expert study of papyrology or the compilation of a Medieval Dictionary.

Far commoner is the other kind of college or university, which is, in fact, an extension of the high school; it exists not for pure but for applied purposeful learning. These institutions are provided by the state or city as a service to the community. They train students for the higher kind of job. The study of English is essential; no one can be effective unless he can express himself in the common tongue. Every student must therefore be taught—to use the current catch phrase—the "arts of communication." On a higher level a more advanced knowledge of English literature is desirable for certain professions where a greater understanding of humanity is required; and it is necessary for teachers in schools, of whom there are a great number in any state. Teachers of English for colleges are also needed, who require other and more specialized training; and finally, a few scholars and critics to leaven the mass. Those who have the honorable vocation to serve in such institutions are greatly privileged; but each kind and level of teaching needs particular abilities and preparation.

There is a general belief—or, to put it more honestly, an agreed pretense—that all members of a Department of English are primarily concerned with research. It is not so; it never has been so. Even in the most austere halls of learning, not one in five of its members is devoted single-mindedly to productive scholarship. A Department of English fulfills its function as it succeeds in producing literate freshmen, eager sophomores, juniors and seniors who are informed common readers, graduates with alert and discriminating minds, instructors who can give form and focus to unformed intelligences, professors who have at least a touch of wisdom and humanity, and scholars who enrich scholarship by their writings.

Where then can the teacher of English begin his labors? "With Freshman Composition," retorts the hardheaded administrator. Yet I pass over this first and most important endeavor, knowing that every publisher of college textbooks will hasten to answer the question with a desk copy of this season's handbook. And besides, our quest is the study and teaching of literature.

Our teacher must first know in his own mind what he is trying to accomplish, which is to create in his students an awareness of what literature is and what it can give them. To become aware the student must learn how to read, and then how to understand what the author is saying, first on the surface, afterward in the subsoil, and finally in the depths.

Civilized literature—English or any other—is a complex growth. As literature accumulates, each successive book owes something to its predecessors; it includes particles and traits from all that have gone before, as we ourselves still bear many traits inherited from past generations, even from our remoter anthropoid ancestors, considerable traces also of primeval slime.

So too the understanding of literature must begin with a knowledge of the elements from which it came. If parents and schoolteachers have so neglected a student that he knows nothing of that body of myth and story which is the warp of all European literature and art, then the instructor must first make up the deficiency. The foundation for study will be an enforced knowledge of the primal stories. And at that the chairman of the Department of English groans, "What! Another course—Pre-Lit I? And yet another instructor to be squeezed into the budget of the Department?"

This is the first dilemma, but not insuperable. Our American system is so rigid that all instruction must be given in standardized courses: M., W., F., at 9, etc. We can hardly hope to break down the hallowed system to suit our own desires. Nor need we, so long as we preserve the outward form for the benefit of registrars and those persons who enter grades on cards. Let us continue to call the thing a course, but merely add a new category to the existing Lecture and Recitation courses called a Reading Course (3 hours).

When occasionally I have made this proposal, I have been met with the objection that students cannot be trusted or expected to read by themselves; if that were true, they should not be studying literature. It is a mistaken judgment; in my experience, our students are eager to be given their freedom from instruction; too often we smother them with our superfluous benevolent supervision.

In a Reading Course—call it Pre-Lit I, if you will—the student is given a list of books to read in which he will find the essential stories—Genesis, Exodus, Joshua, Judges, I & II Samuel, I & II Kings, the four Gospels, and the Acts, and the Apocalypse—a few indeed may already have read some of these —the *Iliad,* the *Odyssey,* the *Aeneid,* Ovid's *Metamorphoses,* some of Plutarch's *Lives.* A second course—Pre-Lit II—might be added for those who major in English Literature: more books of the Bible, Herodotus, Thucydides, Livy, Suetonius, Tacitus, Geoffrey of Monmouth, Malory's *Morte d'Arthur,* and perhaps St. Augustine's *Confessions.*

These narratives call for no exposition, perhaps a very brief introductory comment, but no more; for the student is expected to know only the plain surface content of the books. The instructor therefore is concerned simply with discovering at the end of the semester whether the student has read what is demanded of him. A periodic test asking the simplest questions will suffice: "Who was Jacob's brother? When was Saul also among the prophets? What was the Beast with Seven Heads? On what occasion did Odysseus call himself Nobody? Why is the nightingale called Philomela?" And the administrative savings will be enormous in classroom space and instructor's time. The system might even prove so popular that many courses in literature would become Reading Courses; but that, as yet, is as far away as the Isle of New Atlantis. And before emitting a superior sniff, let any lecturer in an English university draw up a list of fifty similar questions and try them on his students.

Given this skeleton of knowledge, our students must next be taught to read. They learn quickly. In some of our recitation courses, before we fall to discussing a poem, first it is read aloud by one of the students. In the beginning the reading is painfully limp and unintelligible; by the end of the second month they have realized that reading aloud is a joy, for comprehension often comes with the sheer sound of the words. To get the sound, an understanding of the rhythmic pattern is needed, which can be expounded in the terms of prosody—trochees, anapests, initial and medial inversion and the rest—but more easily perceived with the aid of a bongo drum or by tapping on the table.

Thus our sophomore comes to understand a poem in four stages. First, its mere sounds, in themselves a delight; then, a straight comprehension of the surface meaning; then an anatomizing of the verbal devices and images and what they suggest. Now we are ready for the final reading, when once more we read it aloud, but with understanding and delight. This kind of slow-chapped mastication should not be used for every poem; after a few experiments students learn to absorb sound, surface and subsoil meanings at first, or at least second, reading. But the eager instructor should beware of the elementary error of demanding, or even hoping, that his sophomores will find just what he finds in the poem; they will not and cannot because their experience has been different from his.

We can never measure our ultimate success or failure in teaching literature; though we catch glimpses of it in the final examination, when our failures are shown by the student who gives us back just what we have given him, and our success by the student who dares to differ and to reveal ideas of his own. Nor can we triumph in the brilliant students whom we have tried to teach: their success may be the result of our teaching—or in spite of it. Our real successes are not with bright ones but with the inarticulate. Occasionally, years afterward, we hear that we were privileged to bring light to the unseeing, but usually not. The teacher of literature can seldom expect measurable or certain results; he needs an abundance of the three Christian virtues: faith, hope—and charity.

There are other ways of enlightening the sophomore; first, by stimulating his visual imagination. Since sight is the most important of our five senses, literature is largely a record of things seen. The reader needs a knowledge of the shapes of things as they appeared to the author. Doubtless through the movies and comic strips he will have a hazy, inaccurate and incomplete notion of shapes. He needs to acquire a more precise background to his reading by visiting museums and by looking at pictures of buildings, furniture, costume, people, scenery. Such books as the Quennells' *Everyday Things in England* or the series issued by the Boston Art Gallery add large areas of sensitive spots. Imaginative pictures of historical scenes, exact and photographic rather than impressionistic, and dioramas, intelligently constructed, should be in every undergraduate library. And his imagination is further stimulated if he can handle, if not originals, at least good facsimiles of the first versions of the books which he reads—the second quarto of *Hamlet,* the first folio, an issue of Addison's *Spectator,* a manuscript draft of one of Keats' poems, the Ellesmere Chaucer.

And let him be encouraged to read all those things which add to his historic sense—diaries, chronicles, contemporary newspapers, pamphlets, and, above all, letters. Many of the greatest writers have been eager letter writers. Nothing stimulates understanding so much as to read the letters written by an author at the time when he was writing at his best. But these delights should never become a drill. Let the good student know of their existence and how to find them; and then let be. A common and easy error in pedagogy is to be forever instructing; too many of our public parks are spoiled because some zealous expert must tack a name plate on every tree. Education is not cramming heads with facts and theories, but setting a student in the way of making his own discoveries.

It follows that the teacher has many responsibilities. He must himself be what he hopes his students may become; that is, always a student not only of his subject but of life and of those whom he teaches, for the art of teaching lies primarily in understanding what is going on in the heads before him; what they know, how they are thinking, what is new to them, and what this observation will mean to them. One difficulty in our profession is that every year we ourselves know a little more of our subject while each new generation of students starts at the same level. Hence the feeling that this year's batch is always rather worse than its predecessors; which is depressing, until we realize that it is we who have changed.

We have other temptations to be avoided. The first is always to live on, in and for the job. I once knew a Dean who held that unless an instructor could demonstrate by a time chart that he was occupied each week for at least forty hours either in a classroom, or in research, or sitting in a committee, he was an idler and a swindler. A teacher who so spends his time is useless in his profession, for he has forgotten that the word "scholar" comes from a Greek word meaning "leisure." The author of Ecclesiasticus (a book unfortunately excluded from the Protestant canon of the Scriptures) knew better: "The wisdom of a learned man is the fruit of leisure; he must starve himself of doing if he is to come by it" (38:25, Knox translation).

Moreover, scholars and writers do not work regular hours, 9:00 to 5:00. Some prefer to study at midnight; others find their greatest inspiration in a hot bath.

A second and common error is to do too much for our students; this is the same kind of mistake made by a parent who tries to mold his child into an exact copy of himself. In the classroom it takes the form of demanding that the student give back what he has been taught, which may be admirable in the exact sciences, but not in the humanities, where paradoxically the best teacher demands least by way of imitative response, but most by way of private effort. He is a revealer rather than an instructor.

In this meditation I have stressed—maybe overstressed—the fact that for an American reader English literature is foreign. In Biblical studies the expert first considers Palestinian ways and archaeology; and professors of the classics are learned in Greek and Roman antiquities. So also the professor of English must understand the English background. To appreciate Marlowe's plays—and Shakespeare's too, for that matter—and why they caused such excitement, he needs to know about the education given to schoolboys and to undergraduates in the 1570's and 1580's. Wordsworth cannot be completely understood without a knowledge of the North Country where he was reared, Cambridge where he was stimulated as an undergraduate, the left-wing fervor of young students at the time of the French Revolution, the excitement of first reading Godwin's *Political Justice* and the country as he and Dorothy saw it at Alfoxden; those things were more important even than Annette Vallon. To understand Byron, he must be able to sense the attitude of an aristocrat, and especially of one who came into his title by such dubious ways. Then he will realize why Byron and Shelley were naturally attracted to each other, for Shelley belonged to the same class; and why the experiment of bringing Leigh Hunt to Venice was sure to fail. Leigh Hunt was no gentleman, and Mrs. Leigh Hunt was not only shrewish but also infected with all the lower-middle-class disapproval of the aristocracy and its dissolute ways.

Nor have the intangible differences between English and American instincts for life grown less since Byron's time; they are more subtle and less definable. A sensitive instructor, especially one who interprets modern English fiction, will find much to brood over if he gives himself a short course of reading which includes such books as Evelyn Waugh's *Life of Monsignor Ronald Knox,* Christopher Hassall's *A Biography of Edward Marsh,* Algernon Cecil's *House in Bryanston Square*—and Kingsley Amis' *Lucky Jim.*

In all this, the American instructor inevitably finds himself "involved"—to use the jargon. He cannot but loathe certain English attitudes and admire others. In his exposition he ceases to be purely objective and thereby he may suffer scruples, for it is an academic myth that "all teaching must be objective." This is a common fallacy, which ignores human nature. In the exact sciences unemotional objectivity is essential; but in any branch of humane knowledge which concerns thought and behavior, a teacher holds certain beliefs to which he is committed. He cannot be impartial in what he holds dearly. If he believes that he is teaching truth—and he is a dishonest knave if he does not—he is anxious that his students shall perceive it; and he presents his ideas as persuasively as he can. No Catholic can be entirely objective toward Martin Luther, no Baptist toward the Pope, and no Freudian psychologist toward the New Testament.

But the student, however naïve, is not defenseless. On any campus, except a sectarian college which bars all but members of its own sect, there are great divergences of belief; one professor counters another . . . and there are even books in the Library. The honest teacher openly professes his beliefs; but he does not force them upon his students or demand that they accept them, as once a certain professor of anthropology who in a quiz demanded the answer "No" to the question "Has man a soul?" The worst offenders against "objective truth" are usually those agnostics who most loudly demand it. Junior instructors and teaching fellows, especially when passing through the early stages of campus atheism—a malady most incident to young graduates—can also be brutally intolerant.

So much for the more elementary level of the academic teaching of English, which takes up four fifths of the energies of a Department of English.

In his courses for seniors and young graduates, the professor of English is for a large part concerned with those who are soon to become teachers in high schools, whence come later generations of our own students: a heavy responsibility, for deadening, dull teaching of English in the schools has too often originated in pedantic teaching in the university. It is far more important that we produce students to whom literature is a delight than arid scholars and secondhand critics, lest we bring upon ourselves Macbeth's curse—

> *we but teach*
> *Bloody instructions, which being taught return*
> *To plague the inventor.*

The training of the professor-to-be thus calls for certain special attainments, not wholly to be gathered from formal courses. As an undergraduate, he presumably fulfills the usual requirements of specialization in literature with good grades. As victim, he critically observes different professors at work, whose methods he learns to imitate or to avoid; he may even have been brought to realize that the best teachers are not always the easiest or the most popular. A senior graduate on the eve of his doctoral examination observed to me: "The most valuable course I ever had was given by Professor R.; I loathed every minute of it!" As a graduate, he performs his stint of seminars and seminar papers, set out in the proper Modern Language Association style. And then, having at last passed his preliminary examination, he enters into the purgatory of the Ph.D.

The degree of Ph.D. has little to do with philosophy; in certain places it can be gained for embalming or hotel management. But it is the required passport for anyone who aspires to teach in a college or university. As with many other established and indestructible institutions, it is regarded with superstitious reverence; yet it mars more than it makes. The Germans invented it, and it was imported into America at a time when German institutions of learning were rightly, if excessively, admired; but originally it was intended as a method of establishing the capabilities of one who would devote his life to scholarship. The Ph.D. in English is not, as things are, the best kind of preparation for one who will teach English. It is relic of other days and other intentions, comparable to the fetishes of the old-fashioned kind of drill sergeant who still believes that bright buttons, polished boots and precise movement on the parade ground are the only important assets of a fighting soldier.

None of those who taught in the early days of the English schools at Cambridge or elsewhere had achieved the Ph.D. degree, which was not given in the ancient universities until after the First World War, when it was established to attract students from India and other countries who set great value on the title of "Dr." Once established, every candidate for academic appointment in England had thenceforward to obtain it. Higher degrees were regarded not as the essential qualification for a university teacher but, rather, as marks of honor awarded to men who had already established themselves as scholars by notable publications. Nor usually did even famous scholars apply for a higher degree; they waited until it was given them. E. K. Chambers, for one, was still but "B. A. Oxon" when he published his final crowning work—*William Shakespeare: A Study of Facts and Problems.* When he was in his seventies, Oxford finally honored her child with the D. Litt on a public occasion when Chambers represented English letters alongside P. G. Wodehouse.

To win the Ph.D. the aspirant must first write a dissertation on a topic that has not hitherto been fully explored; it must be a "contribution to learning." So many thousands of dissertations have been written and stowed away in university libraries that the choice of topics has become very narrow and specialized. Moreover, established custom and the rigid rules of procedure demand that the writer must demonstrate by means of a bibliography and extensive annotation that he has read every other work remotely relevant to his theme; and every statement must be securely tied to an authority in a footnote set out in the precise formula. By the time he has read all the authorities and extracted (on cards) the relevant citations, he is suffering such acute mental indigestion that he is seldom able to conceive any original thought, and even if he does, he dare not utter it because he cannot quote his authority.

This kind of discipline has its uses as a training for scholars; it fosters enormous energy and discourages wild surmises. But the Ph.D. has also bred a tedious aridity among scholar-critics. Like the painful initiation ceremonies in certain primitive tribes, it must be endured as a prelude for adulthood. It survives because timid administrators demand tangible proofs of ability; unless a man can produce his Ph.D. diploma he cannot prove that he is competent to teach in a university.

Actually, the Ph.D. is as likely to have spoiled him for that honorable vocation. A dissertation on "Some Semantic Aspects of James Joyce's *Ulysses*" or a study of Kenneth Burke's *Lexicon Rhetoricae* is not the best preparation for teaching freshmen to write straight, strong prose. If the aspirant has become fascinated by his research, he will have less patience with teaching humbler minds than his own; if—as happens more often—he has written his dissertation merely because the system demands it, he comes to regard scholarship as a tedious and frustrating waste of time. Neither attitude is desirable. Everyone who would teach in a university needs indeed some firsthand experience of scholarship; but he needs also other assets and experiences which are not to be assessed by any examination. Of these, spiritual experience is most important.

Literature, especially that which communicates in the depths, is directly inspired by spiritual experience. No one can understand Donne—and all modern students must study him—until he has breathed and lived in the same spiritual atmosphere. Donne's poetry is the expression of fierce conflict between sensual and spiritual, between the desire for the certainty of divine union which is the Christian mystic's reward and a despair that he could never attain it. Donne's whole universe was founded on a belief that God is a fact and that Christ is his Son. He was moreover a deep student of theology at a time when a man's theological beliefs might win him the halter of martyrdom or high place in church or state. Until the reader has achieved a sympathetic appreciation, in his heart as well as in his head, of what Donne felt, believed and suffered, he cannot begin to understand what Donne is saying.

Some study of theology (which is not the same as an outline acquaintance with Bible stories) is desirable for any instructor in English literature as a preliminary to its understanding. Moreover, if he has received no religious instruction in youth, he may learn to his surprise that the religious faith of some of his maturer students is not just adolescent emotion but founded on hard reason. Such knowledge guards him against brash intolerance; and it is essential for anyone who studies and expounds medieval literature.

Chaucer lived in a pre-Renaissance, pre-Reformation Catholic world. He was no saint; though he had the keenest perception of fraud and hypocrisy, he recognized sanctity when he saw it. He was a great reader and at the same time a man of the world, surprisingly modern in his outlook and his sense of humor. But, unlike most modern writers, he was not tormented by everlasting doubts and introspection because he believed that his church was divinely founded to teach and preserve the truth: there was no more to say. The Chaucerian expert cannot understand Chaucer's world until he too has to some extent experienced it. As a whole, that kind of world no longer exists; but he can find considerable fragments in some of the remote civilizations—in South America and in the Far East—where life is still lived with primitive equipment and in a predemocratic environment. He can also find a Catholic civilization not too far from home, no farther than Quebec Province, but he should travel beyond Montreal and Quebec city, into the country districts and the small towns. He needs to speak French; but presumably he is already familiar with that tongue. Further, a month spent in a Benedictine monastery can teach him much. He will be very welcome. He can hear liturgical chant at its best; and if he confers with the Director of Theology he may even catch a glimpse of an order of being not hitherto realized. Too many medievalists regard the Middle Ages with the kind of objective condescending curiosity that one bestows upon a small tank of tropical fish.

The training of a professor of English should also include some direct experience of the writing and publication of books, not merely the scholarly volume which a university press reluctantly publishes at the author's expense, but books intended for sale to the common reader. In this way he comes to realize the facts of literary life, and that authors, great and small, need a knowledge of hard economic laws. Before the finished work can be judged and labeled by the hierophants, the author must first satisfy a publisher that his book is worth publishing; and then he must learn about literary contracts, and his own rights and obligations, for a book can be a valuable property in most unexpected ways and for many years. A little manual intended as an introduction to the reading of Shakespeare carries British and American rights, translation rights, anthology rights, broadcasting and television rights, even if it is unlikely to be converted into a drama, a film or a phonograph record.

Nor are these sordid details irrelevant to the art or the history of literature, for authors take great satisfaction in their rewards. Dr. Johnson once declared that no man but a blockhead ever wrote, except for money. At a gathering of authors, the talk turns less on the objective correlative or other obscure principles than on royalties, the generosity of publishers, the competence of literary agents, paperback rights and the strange tastes of the common reader. Shakespeare himself was concerned with such matters; he took great pains to woo his public by humble epilogues, even if—in private moments—he had distressing reactions against public means which public manners breeds.

An academic who seeks what the taxgatherer calls "gainful self employment" must likewise woo the common reader, or at least that section of common readers who are interested in what he can offer. The experience will correct many of the false and fantastic notions which he has imbibed from his professor of critical theory.

In more optimistic days I had wild, unfulfilled hopes that I might become, if not rich, at least comfortable by writing novels, short stories and plays. I wrote fifteen short stories of which half a dozen were printed, but at an average reward of £5 apiece; and five novels, of which one (an adventure story) was published with mild success; and five plays (two tragedies, two comedies, and one historical play). Of these one was accepted by the Cambridge Repertory Theatre for fall production; but the Theatre folded in August. Another was to be produced in London—"if there is no crisis"—and Neville Chamberlain went to Munich. And a third a famous actress would have taken, but her management refused. After that, creative writing seemed rather a waste of effort; but, like the sons of the old man who bade them dig for treasure in his vineyard, I did gather my reward: I learned from practical experience that the processes of creation are very different from the theories of the critics—on which mystery a reading of Somerset Maugham's *The Summing Up* lets in the sunlight of experience.

Another practical asset to be sought is the acting and directing of plays. In my preparatory school each December a handful of parents suffered from the Christmas play—a straight version in dismal doggerel of one of the well-known fairy tales. Being fair skinned I was chosen to enact the heroine—the Princess in *Aladdin,* and Fatima in *Bluebeard,* and on a special occasion Alice in *The Mad Tea-party.*

More rewarding and mature were certain efforts with the King's College, London, Dramatic Society, of which the first was a production of *Love's Labor's Lost.* The Society could not afford to hire costumes and so decided to produce the play in modern dress. They invited J. Isaacs, later Professor of English Literature at the University of London and a much-esteemed contributor to the B.B.C. Third Programme, and myself to direct. We set the scene in the garden of a country house, with a statue of Cupid (borrowed from a ladies' underwear shop in the Strand) as centerpiece. We clothed the young men in blazers and white flannels (then worn in the country), and the girls in summer frocks. The Curate was made up to look like the Professor of Pastoral Theology and played by one of his students; and the whole affair went with such swing and hilarity that we were accused of gagging the sacred text. Actually, though we had cut some of the obscure jokes which not even professors understand, not a word was added. The play had also one unforeseen advantage; the Princess was played by a lady called Eileen (later better known as Greer) Garson.

Fired by this success the Society next embarked on *Othello,* also in modern dress. The scene was now set in North Africa, with Italian uniforms for the men and modern costume for the women. Desdemona made a magnificent first entry wearing an evening cloak. Iago was presented as a stocky ex-sergeant with three rows of campaign ribbons, while Cassio was a dapper staff officer with a breast bare of decorations. This production moved one professional London drama critic to declare that modern costume was the only way for Shakespeare: for the first time he had seen *Othello* as a play about real people and not as a fancy-dress ritual. As directors our problem was not to probe for underlying symbols or even to illustrate the iterative imagery, but to persuade the audience that this Desdemona was the kind of girl who would have made this Othello mad, first with love, and then with a killing jealousy; which was Shakespeare's problem also.

During my years in Canada the Queen's Drama Guild began to put on Shakespeare. Hitherto the Guild had preferred Broadway farce, but very timidly they ventured on *Twelfth Night.* During the rehearsals one player was overheard to say incredulously to another, "Did you realize that this is a good play?" The next production was *Hamlet,* where we had the unusual advantage of having Hamlet played by a young man of twenty, uncontaminated by any previous sight of the play acted by a star performer. In this production I was able to try out certain theories of my own that Hamlet is not a hypersensitive graduate but vigorous, impetuous, full blooded.

The chance of sharing in a production may not come to every instructor but at least he should see every possible performance of great drama, especially when acted by professionals.

When at last he has achieved his Ph.D. the young instructor receives his first appointment. Quite early he is made aware that the successful academic (that is, one marked out for promotion and advancement) must be a good teacher, a productive scholar, a zealous committee man, a keen supporter of community culture in the form of lectures, concerts and plays, and a regular patron of student activities on the campus and in the stadium. The smaller the institution, the more insistent these demands. And he may well wonder how to combine these irreconcilable elements. How can he starve himself of doing when he is so stuffed with activity?

Good teaching is very laborious, especially in our academic system. For three or four courses, thrice weekly for fifteen successive weeks, the instructor must try to stimulate the same audiences. It calls not only for inexhaustible energy and a quick mind, but long planning and a considerable gift for showmanship. Over the years, the teacher saves himself much unnecessary labor if he plans thoroughly and wisely. Full notes for every lecture or demonstration, carefully, even elaborately prepared, and then stored away with a brief comment on how each went over provides ammunition for years—not that he should be still giving the same lecture twenty years after—yet at any time he may be suddenly called upon to take the place of a sick colleague; if he can then draw out the appropriate packet of notes he is saved hectic midnight preparations.

This kind of planning keeps the young instructor busy for several years, for usually it takes three years to shape a new course into a unity. At first delivery lectures seldom have quite the expected result. Some run too short—a nightmare for the beginner who finds himself with ten minutes to go and only two minutes' more matter; wise teachers always include an emergency section in their notes. Others run too long, which is less of a problem. Some evoke the wrong response, laughter at times in what was meant to be pathetic or moving; one must always be ready for that emergency. And then there is the incalculable, ever-shifting atmosphere of the classroom, affected by so many intangibles—the class bore or the class rebel, or general fatigue after a social weekend, or the depression arising from continual dull bad weather, or the sudden stimulus of a bright day; all these unpredictables the instructor must be ready to surmount.

Meanwhile he will have been made aware by the chairman of his department that publications are expected. This hotly debated matter of scholarly publication needs more objective examination than it usually receives; both those who demand it and those who resent it have their case.

A College President, and his myrmidons the Dean and the Chairman of the Department, are rightly concerned that all faculty members show a reasonable and competent zeal, for though the learned man needs leisure, it can too easily degenerate into sloth, which is the deadly sin most common to academics, especially after they have reached security of tenure. Books, articles, reviews indicate that the professor is still "active"; they give measurable results which can be listed in the annual report. But the demand for such achievements can also encourage enormous hypocrisy, for the published works are seldom read by administrative officials; and a long list sometimes includes some very trivial "contributions." Besides, the demand for learned articles as a necessary prelude to promotion has caused publications to flood upon us until we are overwhelmed by what we have evoked. A good broadcast talk over the campus radio is more valuable to the university, the subject and the public than half a dozen reluctant articles in a learned journal.

The fiat of "no promotion before publication" can be

grossly unfair. A young instructor who has not as yet established his name finds it very difficult to plant an article, however brilliant. Every learned journal receives ten offers for one which it can print. Even if the article is accepted, a year or more may pass before it appears. And as for a book, no commercial publisher nowadays can afford to print many academic works. Most authors must therefore turn to a University Press, which sometimes requires heavy payment. If lucky he may win a grant from some fund; if not, he must borrow from his friends in the hope that the investment will bring promotion and increased salary.

This demand for publications is yet another example of the commonest of modern superstitions: nothing is valuable unless it can be measured.

Skill in teaching and in scholarship are different kinds of activity. Both demand a man's full energy. If the university desires good teaching above everything, then the good teacher should be recognized, rewarded and promoted for his skill. A good teacher needs to be a great reader, a lively talker, and interested in everything, especially people; probably also he will be a fine host, and a welcome guest. If he spends much of his time going around, and in talk, even in cocktail bars, he is all the while collecting pearls which afterward he dispenses to his students. So long as he remains a good teacher, the university should rejoice in his gifts in the classroom and not fuss over how he spends his time outside, so long as he fulfills Polonius' demand that it is not open to incontinency or other scandal. When I was a young academic, a wise man (who afterward became Dean of St. Paul's) said to me, "You must make up your mind whether you will be a reading man or a writing man; you can't be both." The great teacher is usually a reading man.

Contrariwise, the scholar is a writing man, and writing consumes much time. He must be something of a recluse; his reading is always for a purpose and therefore narrow. Though there are a few notable exceptions to the rule, great scholars are seldom good teachers, for that single-minded devotion to true research demands a narrowing of interest and a neglect of irrelevant activity. Scholarship of this kind is hardly possible on the campus of a "teaching" university, where the professor's time is so much occupied with lectures, and classes, and seminars, interviews with students, reading of essays and blue books, and the direction of theses, even if he is not also member of several committees. Even the most fortunate have long clutter periods each year when for weeks on end they are kept away from their research. It follows that if a university wishes to include great scholars on its faculty, they must be treated rather as "resident artists" who are encouraged to pursue their work in their own way. In European universities, where scholarship is more highly regarded, the professor is seldom expected to appear in the classroom more often than five hours a week, in some places even less.

To all of which the Dean of the Faculty of Arts replies, "Granted. But to justify the promotion either of a good teacher or a good scholar, I must have something to show the President. Every department competes for more than its proper share of the budget. What evidence can you offer that your candidate is as good as you claim?"

This is a very real problem, not to be brushed aside angrily by good teachers who are suffering from a sense of neglected worth, or even by young instructors whose appointments lapse at the end of three years. While the good men are recognized within their own departments, how can their worth be demonstrated outside in an academic society dominated by sociologists and psychologists with their graphs, statistics and tables?

The annual bibliography of faculty publications has no value unless a committee of Patient Persons is formed to read and assess the worth of each. Other systems have been tried. One is known as "faculty evaluation." It was inspired, presumably, by the communist practice of encouraging the young to spy and report on their elders, but put into respectable form by experts in pedagogic sociology. Periodically elaborate forms are issued to all students on which they are invited to record anonymously their opinions of each professor and his courses. When these forms have been collected and submitted to processing, they are read by Deans, Chairmen of Departments, and lastly by the teacher himself, who is expected to amend his ways in the light of these revelations. This method is of little positive value and often quite harmful. Since the reports are anonymous, there is no way of knowing whether the writer is responsible or disgruntled. Sensitive instructors are bitterly hurt by brutal criticism; nor are students capable of assessing any but the most obvious shortcomings or virtues of their instructors, for the true value of a course cannot be perceived until long afterward. It also encourages the more plausible teachers to play for popularity.

However, if the administration really believes in the system, then it should logically be extended. The members of a department should report anonymously on their Chairman to the Dean; the Chairmen of Departments should report on the Dean to the President; the Deans in turn on the President to the Governing Body; and since the Governors themselves are representatives of the public, the administrators should express their anonymous opinions to the public through the press, which would certainly co-operate.

There is, however, another and far more valid method of assessing a teacher's powers. In other countries at the end of the course students are examined by external examiners who have not been responsible for their teaching. Examinations of this kind must be conducted by those who are themselves experienced teachers of English—the objective methods of right/wrong questions are quite useless. At least two independent examiners are needed for each comprehensive examination, and the process must be leisurely; it cannot be rushed through in seventy-two hours so that the candidate may graduate next Saturday. The results of such an examination reveal how well the students have been taught. However, this method, though not entirely unknown, is so rare in our American system, that it is hardly worth pursuing.

In spite of the shortcomings of College Presidents and Chairmen of Departments, few professors of English willingly exchange the life for other more lucrative activities. We make our necessary genuflection in the House of Rimmon (adjoining the President's office in the Administration Building), and we go our own ways with a freedom denied to our more prosperous neighbors. And, unless our minds and hearts harden, we continue to learn the art all the time, and most of all from our own students.

4 ✦ *Publications*

The author of *Red Brick University* is so eager that all academics shall be mainly occupied in research that he would even abolish the much cherished privilege of life tenure enjoyed by professors and associate professors (called in England "readers"), for he has observed that when a man is appointed professor he seems too often to lose his former zeal for high scholarship: let him therefore live always in a state of fear lest in his fifties he be cast into unemployment; that will keep the sluggard busy till the end!

It would appear that Bruce Truscot had not himself been head of a large department or he would have experienced that sapping of energy which is the fate of every conscientious chairman as he is slowly drained white (like a flea-infested hen) by faculty and senate meetings, committees, syllabuses, conferences, writing of testimonials, correspondence and interviews with candidates for employment, consultations with graduates, examinations, departmental quarrels, and the unavoidable social and public functions at which he must represent his department. No one of these in itself seems too strenuous, but cumulatively they debilitate. So burdensome are the demands that any chairman who produces serious scholarship is patently neglecting his duty; as indeed many of them do (especially in England) by casting their administrative responsibilities on a second in command. It is as well to be clear-eyed about "publications."

"Published work" records different kinds and degrees of activity. The first and most rewarding is true research, which leads to the discovery of new facts and so adds to knowledge. In his heart of hearts every scholar hopes that by some miracle of lucky insight he may ultimately find a few pages of the original manuscript of *Hamlet* or the quarto of *Love's Labor's Won*. And indeed several discoveries almost as exciting have been made in the last sixty years. They may happen anywhere. Partly they are just luck; more often they are the rewards of an alert mind quick to realize the significance of something seen, inspired serendipity.

Certain sites are most likely to yield results. Doubtless there are bundles of manuscripts in the Folger or the Huntington Libraries still to be examined and calendared; and there are many private collections in England and elsewhere which might produce anything; the Boswell papers lay untouched at Malahide for more than a century. But the Public Record Office in London is the largest repository of secrets still uncovered. It holds, for example, the papers of many thousands of cases which were brought before Queen Elizabeth I's Court of Star Chamber and have lain undisturbed since. Shakespeare's deer stealing may yet come to light.

Research into these records requires not only long training, intricate knowledge of legal procedures and court Latin, and the skill to decipher execrable handwriting, but a special ability to interpret what has been found--a gift not always bestowed on expert researchers. However, this kind of research is the most satisfying of all, illustrated, for example, in C. J. Sisson's *Lost Plays of Shakespeare's Age,* in his reconstruction of Chapman's lost play *The Old Joiner of Aldgate* and the whole disreputable story of Agnes Howes' unhappy legacy, which is not only good reading in itself but adds much to our knowledge of playmaking at the end of the sixteenth century. Researchers in the P.R.O. belong as it were to a very exclusive club, to which a young instructor with a grant for a year's study is not likely to qualify for admittance. Research of this kind is very slow and laborious but essential to most creative scholarship.

Great works of scholarship are rare, for they are the result of an exceptional combination of gifts. A scholar in English needs vast miscellaneous knowledge, including Greek, Latin, French and possibly also German, Italian, Spanish and Hebrew, a comprehensive and accurate memory, a perceptive and alert mind, enormous energy and industry, indefatigable perseverance, a sense of vocation which cannot be turned aside, freedom from personal strains and worries, and not least the gift of common sense, without which he degenerates into a sterile perfectionist who knows everything but can never bring himself to finish a book. A scholar of this kind needs special encouragement. He can hardly survive in the atmosphere of a teaching university.

Nevertheless the young instructor who is adequately gifted and ambitious to become a scholar need not be too despondent, so long as he is willing to face the cost. He can expect no cash reward, and the more scholarly his attainments, the fewer are those who can appreciate their value; his joy's soul lies in the doing. And even if he cannot hope to become one of the very select company with Spedding, McKerrow, Greg, Simpson, Lovejoy, Lowes and their peers, he can seek an honorable place in the second rank. Much depends on the way he uses his opportunities as an apprentice when he compiles his Ph.D. dissertation.

To most graduates the choice of the topic for the dissertation is difficult, because they lack a sense of direction and reality. The best topics have long since been mined; there remain only the slag heaps of former explorers. The few who aspire to become scholars are often prematurely ambitious, and the many who are more eager for the needed diploma are satisfied if they can find something (preferably in modern fiction or criticism) which will pass the doctoral committee. Yet even with the best, the Ph.D. dissertation is seldom an important piece of scholarship; it lacks maturity of learning and of experience of life. An aspirant should therefore avoid any topic which demands vast and comprehensive erudition, or he is in great danger of never ending his search. He should remember that his dissertation is apprentice work, and he gains most if he acquires wide general knowledge and an experience of scholarly methods in the doing.

For this reason, when asked by a puzzled graduate to suggest topics for his dissertation, I usually advise him to consider editing a text, either a play or some work of like length—a hundred pages or so. Since most of the best plays have already been edited, he must choose one of the less important. No great harm is done if the results are second rate; too many good topics have been spoiled by premature dissertations, especially in the 1920's. In the course of editing, he studies perforce many other plays, literary history and criticism, historical background, stage history, biography, and the principles of modern textual criticism, and he amasses much miscellaneous knowledge in collecting material for his notes. A supreme advantage of this kind of topic is that it has a predictable end. Large and generous projects may seem more valuable, but often they prove interminable. In the course of his editing the aspirant sometimes encounters certain lacks—books which have not yet been written, or adequately edited, or which need rewriting. Here is his chance for useful publication.

A young academic who would then break into print faces many problems. Long ago a Cambridge man described them feelingly in a play called *The Pilgrimage to Parnassus,* in which the two heroes (or victims) are appropriately named Studioso and Philomusus. Both are still with us; Studioso hopes to become a scholar, Philomusus is drawn toward the critics. In the 1960's they have a far greater choice of jobs in colleges and universities than ever before but less opportunity for free publication because the economics of publishing have so entirely changed in the last twenty-five years.

Before the Second World War, publishers, at least in England, could afford to produce a book which was likely to sell no more than a thousand copies and to offer the author an advance of royalty on its sales which would enable him to pay his typist and still be remunerated on the same scale as an unskilled road worker. Costs of typesetting, paper and binding have grown so high that few publishers dare now be so venturesome.

On the other hand, fellowships for study, sabbatical leave, and grants in aid of publication are now generally available; no scholarly work of merit need perish. The chances of publication are thus at first sight as good as they ever were, but with certain important differences. When the writer received a modest reward in cash, he wrote for the delight of the common reader, or at least for that smaller circle of common readers who were also interested in scholarly matters. The recipient of a grant-in-aid is no longer concerned with common readers but solely with earning the esteem of his colleagues who have recommended him for the reward. Thus it comes to pass that academic writers compose academic books for academic readers and they suffer from that constriction of the arteries which is the vocational hazard of all who appeal only to the coterie.

What hopes of literary fame then remain for Studioso and Philomusus? If Studioso is indeed endowed with the scholar's attributes there are still many openings for definitive works of scholarship, great and small. No complete or adequate edition has appeared for more than fifty years of the Elizabethan sonneteers, or the poems of John Davis, or the plays of John Dryden. A little research in *The Cambridge Bibliography of English Literature* or in the bibliographies of the Oxford *History of English Literature*—in Douglas Bush's excellent survey of the early seventeenth century, for instance—soon reveals authors even of the first rank whose works are unobtainable. Some of these, Studioso may find already listed in *PMLA* and elsewhere as "work in progress," which is often no more than what the bibliographers call a "blocking entry"—a claim pegged out to keep others off. If on inquiry he finds that "progress" should more accurately read "remote prospect" he need not be deterred.

If he then chooses to devote himself—using the word "devote" in its fullest sense—to a definitive edition of works that are worth reviving, he should first, as an act of preliminary prudence, find a patron (which nowadays means a Foundation) to ensure publication. Then he must decide whether he will labor for the benefit of scholars, or of common readers, or of student readers (who are in the middle class, more exacting in their interests than common readers and less erudite than scholars). Each class needs a different kind of text and treatment.

The common reader's interest is in the book itself and what it says. He needs a text which makes for easy reading; uncouth spelling and unfamiliar format irritate him. He has small interest in conflicting texts and variant readings. He looks for a commentary and an introduction to illuminate the work as humane literature, and notes which are complete in themselves; it is neither help nor kindness to refer him to "RES, xxvii, 77" for further illuminations. He reads for pleasure in his armchair; he should not be expected to interrupt his reading while he proceeds to the periodical room of the university library.

The scholar's needs are incalculable and unpredictable. Often he is not even interested in the content of a book. A zealot for textual study is fascinated by irregular spellings, inconsistent speech headings and those typographical peculiarities which madden the common reader. No text but the original can ever satisfy him, though he may temporize with microfilm or a collotype facsimile; but he condemns any cheaper process. When the Yale University Press published its reduced facsimile of the First Folio in a line process at a low price, the textual experts condemned it with loathing. "This process is inadequate," they cried; "give us collotype." But collotype is so expensive that no publisher could afford it.

The student reader, however, is less exacting and more rewarding; he buys the Yale facsimile in thousands, for the edition is good enough for any normal reader who is concerned with content and literary value. Yet he shares many of the scholar's interests. He demands therefore that a topical or literary allusion be explained so that he may more fully understand what he is reading. He is interested also in the author, his life, his environment, his methods and his sources, and even the varieties of his text. The most worthwhile edition is therefore one which satisfies the student, and preferably without repelling the common reader.

Accordingly, Studioso should preface his labors with a general meditation on the fundamental differences between scholarship and pedantry. Humility, he will discover, is the mark of scholarship. Great scholars know their own limitations and admit them. They serve the reader with their learning. Contrariwise, pedantry is a form of pride, for the pedant is less concerned to share his knowledge than to advertise his own superiority.

From the ethics and metaphysics of scholarship, Studioso next looks for models to imitate, specimens of notable editing. There are several, such as Percy Simpson's Oxford *Jonson,* F. E. Hutchinson's edition of *The Works of George Herbert,* H. J. C. Grierson's *The Poems of John Donne,* Fredson Bowers' edition of Dekker's plays. Each offers certain lessons.

The Oxford *Jonson* was long in gestation. Newborn chins grew rough, razorable and grizzled between the first announcement and the final performance. For those who lived long enough to acquire the eleventh volume, the result was a magnificent example of scholarship, well planned, complete, finely printed. And the text would have gladdened Ben Jonson by so exactly carrying out his notions of what a play text should be; nevertheless, the text is difficult for the student, or indeed any reader, because Ben himself was somewhat of a pedant. He insisted on printing his plays in the old classical manner, with inadequate stage directions (which seldom even note exits and entrances), and the maddening convention of starting a new scene with each entry. The student who would fully relish Jonson needs the Oxford *Jonson;* but for easy reading or an acting version he must look elsewhere.

Yet the Oxford *Jonson* is a fine example of the art of editing, of which the test is that whenever the reader needs help in understanding the text, he finds it. Simpson never fails him; indeed he gives such good measure that sometimes the reader is beguiled away from his reading, fascinated by the commentary. To achieve such a result an editor must become almost a reincarnation of his author, entering into his mind and understanding how it functions. He needs vast imaginative sympathy. Ben was learned; his learning must be illustrated; and the editor must be as learned as he. Ben also had keen eyes and ears; he was, in the words of a contemporary, "a mere empyric, one that gets what he hath by observation." His plays have thus the immediacy of a newsreel; they record the latest gossip, fashion and catchword; these things too need illustrating by an editor who can project himself into Jonson's world. That also calls for learning but of another kind.

Compared with Jonson, George Herbert is simple. He was at times a metaphysical poet; his thoughts are obliquely expressed and need paraphrase; and he was so saturated with the Bible that he thinks in its language. This too—and especially for the modern reader—needs demonstration. Hutchinson's edition is a model of helpful learning which unobtrusively leads the reader into Herbert's mind.

Donne is the most difficult of the three, as he was the most learned. Grierson's edition of Donne's poems is monumentally erudite: no reference or allusion to the Early Fathers seems to have escaped him; but yet Grierson was strangely negligent of the student reader's needs. He notes that "The Éxtasie" "is one of the most important of the lyrics of Donne's metaphysic of love, of the interconnection and mutual dependence of body and soul," but he throws no light on the meaning of its many difficult lines and phrases. The student reader still lacks a definitive edition of Donne's poems.

Fredson Bowers' *Dramatic Works of Thomas Dekker* is the latest example of what some modern scholars regard as the right way of editing. Its textual apparatus is so elaborate that more than a quarter of the pages (and of the cost of production) are concerned with such matters as variant readings between different states of a quarto, formes, foul papers, pied type, and the rest. In printing the text, the editor has kept eccentricities of spelling, which is altered "as little as possible," but he has made speech headings consistent, reverted to the old eighteenth-century convention of indenting a part line which continues or completes a full line of verse, normalized the use of capitals, corrected mislineations and generally tidied up the original. The result is a text as acceptable as the student reader can hope to find, but useless for the scholar who needs a text uncontaminated by editorial zeal. Moreover Bowers is interested only in the text; no help is, apparently, to be given to the reader. There is neither historical introduction nor commentary, no gloss, no attempt to elucidate difficult phrases or to explain allusions. Henceforward, it would appear, scholarly editors are to be concerned only with textual matters; the meaning of what an author wrote is of no importance. There thus seems to be considerable danger lest English scholarship be perverted into an arcane textuality comprehensible only to Past Masters of the Grand Lodge of Hermetic Bibliographers. If so, this admirable edition is a portent of disaster. The first distemper of learning, Bacon observed, is "when men study words and not matter"; what would he have said of that study which is concerned not with the mind of the author but with the vagaries of his printer?

Philomusus has other ambitions. He is somewhat repelled by the drudgery of minute scholarship and prefers to study ideas or individuals. He too has many illustrious examples for imitation, from Arthur Lovejoy's *The Great Chain of Being* to C. S. Lewis's *The Allegory of Love*. There are excitements in this kind of study which demands wide leisurely reading but little minute scratching in records.

Attractive as all these projects may be, few of them satisfy the greatest immediate need both of Studioso and Philomusus —*money!* Without it, neither can wholeheartedly apply himself to scholarly or critical work, especially in the earlier years when a young academic is most eager and ambitious. Compared with the rewards of medicine, law or mechanical engineering, humane learning is meagerly sustained. The instructor is thus forced to add to his income in some way, and the commonest is by undertaking extension or summer teaching whereby he sacrifices to immediate necessity his small surplus of time and energy. This cruel dilemma wrecks many, especially those who marry young, the cold hard fact of life being that a wife and children are impediments to great enterprises.

One form of authorship which can be gratifyingly profitable is the composition of textbooks for college students, though competition is keen and brutal; successful textbooks are ruthlessly and unscrupulously imitated, especially those which have vast potential sales, above all for such courses as freshman composition.

The writing of a college textbook demands certain skills in the compiler, who is bound within rigid limits. His books must be suitable for already established courses, and be better than the existing textbook; he can hardly hope that, however brilliant his production, any department will prescribe a new course solely that students may have a chance of using his book, unless perchance he is a professor of enormous reputation in a vast university. He requires, therefore, a certain sense of what will stimulate students and not less of what will appeal to their instructors. An instructor who has a new notion can be sure that it will be carefully and sympathetically judged by publishers, especially the more prosperous and reputable, who are eager hunters after new ideas and authors. And he should always be ready to share the risk by taking a royalty on sales rather than an outright payment. The publisher's investment, even in a simple book, is considerable; the author risks only losing his wasted time. Besides, if the book succeeds, he draws a pleasant income for many years without further effort. He should, however, regard the writing of textbooks as a form of supplementary income wherewith he buys leisure for scholarly but unprofitable labors of love. The two forms of activity are complementary, each enhancing the other. It is good for scholars to have close contact with simpler and less erudite minds, and the best textbooks are usually written by those with firsthand experience as scholars and as authors.

Teachers of English have other opportunities, which some of them take. There is an abiding interest in the lives of authors. Philomusus can turn to biography, which is a rewarding form of critical scholarship, and can be pursued on various levels. On the grand scale—Richard Ellmann's *James Joyce* is a recent example—biography requires considerable leisure, the handsome backing of a fund, travel, and easy access to collections of letters and other material. If the subject is a popular author, the biographer is sure of readers and of a publisher; with great luck he may even be chosen by the Book-of-the-Month Club. Works of this kind have their special difficulties. A good biography is a portrait, not a passport photograph. The biographer also needs special graces—a keen intuitive understanding of character, minute instinctive perception of the atmosphere in which his subject lived—the sense almost of the smell of his dining room—and the ability to convey it.

Biographies of a contemporary are the most difficult to write, for not only is the material immense but many readers have already fixed impressions. They will judge the work as fiercely as one judges the likeness in the oil portrait of a friend. The biographer too has the difficult problem of what to select and how to present it. A collection of extracts or précis of letters, thinly glued together with a running commentary, can be very dull reading. Yet if the biographer tells the story in his own words, the result may seem a distortion. He faces also the problem of length, for, as Aristotle so sagely observed, beauty depends on magnitude and order; an exceedingly small picture cannot be beautiful, nor one of vast size. The best biography therefore is not necessarily the longest. There is indeed a limit to what we may wish to read even about James Joyce. Here again the biographer must decide whether he is creating a work of art which conveys an impression, or compiling a fat dossier of information from which the reader may make his own judgment. Both kinds have their uses.

If Philomusus is less ambitious, he may content himself with a critical study of an author or of one or more of his works, *The Four Quartets,* maybe, or *Daisy Miller.* This kind of work has several advantages; it demands little research; most of it can be written in comfort at home. The result is not so much a demonstration of the permanent meaning of *The Four Quartets* (for, as has already been shown, there is no permanent meaning) as a self-portrait of "Mr. Philomusus reading *The Four Quartets.*" Actually, criticism often tells us more of the critic than of the criticized; as we learn so much of Matthew Arnold from his observations on Wordsworth, Keats, Shelley and Chaucer.

Great critics are even rarer than great scholars, and their works less permanent, for they interpret literature for their contemporaries, whose tastes are ever inconstant. The few who are read after two generations survive by reason of a certain greatness of personality which transcends their writing. Yet, unless he has an inordinate desire for posthumous fame, Philomusus need not be deterred from writing works of criticism. Certainly he is a more effective teacher if he can speak with authority based on published, and therefore publicly assailable, work. However, unless he has something original to offer, he will be well advised to keep close watch on current fashions, for critics as a body follow the "trends" as eagerly as ambitious local politicians attach themselves to the presidential candidate's motorcade. The present fashion for tracing the influence of the *Summa Theologica* and the doctrine of Grace is almost worked out; typology has still some years to run.

If the writing of a book is beyond his reach, Philomusus is reduced to the annual article in a critical or learned journal. Custom calls him to it, and he cannot resist the official demand for "publication." Learned articles are usually the least profitable of all, oppressing him that gives and him that takes; they are groans of desperation, chunks hewn from a dissertation. On the few occasions when a writer has something fresh and pressing to say, and writes with zest and enthusiasm, his article stands out like a candle in the dark, a good deed in a naughty world.

Another reason for the dullness of so many short pieces is that too few academic writers have had enough experience of writing. A good writer, like a good pianist, needs daily practice and a love of the art for its own sake. To keep in practice, he must write his weekly minimum of 3,000 to 5,000 words. And it is good for his ego if he is rewarded for his labors. An occasional fee, or, better, the six-monthly royalty check, is a great incentive to creative work; a hundred dollars earned by writing is ultimately more valuable than a thousand made by extension teaching.

Authorship is a profession, whether the writer be poet, novelist, playwright, critic, scholar, biographer, essayist or even compiler of textbooks. A professional writer needs a threefold personality; he must be creator, finding vast satisfaction in forcing words to express his exact meaning; critic, to appraise his own creation with cold and hostile judgment; and common reader whom he tries to please. It is a fair test of an author's ability that someone is ready to buy his wares. Indeed, it can reasonably be argued that unless they are salable, they are not worth printing. At which the editors of learned and critical reviews cry out indignantly: "We can never hope to pay our authors; without a handsome subsidy we could not even exist."

"Learned and critical journals: their functions and justification" is a profitable subject for inquiry. Such journals serve scholars and critics in much the same way as a trade journal serves its industry. The scholar and the critic has each his own specialized interests which mean little to the common reader; and they need an exchange where new discoveries and ideas can be displayed and discussed. But the supply of discoveries and new ideas which are worth reporting is far less than the space available for their display; and the pages of the journal must be filled. Moreover, editors are flooded with contributions from those who must publish something somewhere. This pressure is so great that every few months a new journal is started to provide fresh outlet for the desperate, with the result that English studies have so proliferated that no one scholar can any longer keep level even with the bibliography of his own sub-specialty. We have almost reached the stage where no professor can claim to be familiar with Shakespeare; he can only hope to be regarded as an expert on the quartos of *Much Ado About Nothing.*

Such profusion will overwhelm English studies unless checked by one of two drastic measures: either an agreed limit shall be set on the numbers of books and articles to be published each year—which would require a panel of judges and selectors; or the publication every ten years of an authoritative list of "books and articles worth reading"—all others to be disregarded, even by thesis writers. Neither proposal is very practicable! The simpler solution is to persuade administrators that only those who have a vocation for authorship should be encouraged to follow it. If ever it became an established principle to discourage the publication of any but the first quality, then a variety of problems would be solved. The number of learned journals would diminish, together with demands on shelf room in the university library; the quality of books and articles published would be enhanced; and good teachers would have more time for private reading and greater encouragement to improve their teaching.

They manage these things better in New Atlantis.

5 ✦ *Departments of English*

In the expanding universe of the 1960's, a young instructor, his new Ph.D. hood still snug upon his shoulders, has many openings. Even if his academic attainments are mediocre, by the end of August some desperate chairman will hire him to teach freshman composition. If he should be one of the brighter stars, highly commended by influential professors, the world is all before him—or at least he usually has some choice between a small college or a vast state university: a nice choice, for in both the gains and losses are equally balanced.

A small college with its student body of about two thousand, is a happy band of brothers, eager torchbearers for humanity. Its Department of English is small, less than a score in number; the college spirit is keen; the community close knit. Life in such an Arcadia can be very rewarding; and (I am told) colleges of this kind do exist. But before he signs his contract the prudent applicant will do marvelous wisely if he make inquiry of the true state of the community, preferably from those of junior or middle rank in the department. Sometimes a small college seethes with bitter rivalries and personal rancors; elementary teaching of indifferent students is an excessive burden; opportunities for private study are very limited, and there is little if any work with graduates.

In such conditions the aspiring scholar is seldom stimulated either by his students or by his colleagues, few of whom have a special knowledge of his particular kind. A man can soon atrophy in the complacent isolation of a small college. Unless he keeps up his contact with his peers elsewhere, he is too easily tempted to channel his energies into the drama society, the college orchestra, bridge, faculty feuds and politics, or cocktail parties.

There are other dangers and disadvantages. The smaller the college, the greater can be the outside interference of the local benefactor, and the smothering influence of outstanding personalities—an autocratic president (or, even worse, his intriguing wife), a long-established treasurer, or some cantankerous senior professor whose whims must be everlastingly humored. Moreover, many small departments of English are dominated by an elderly she-dragon (as fearsome as any encountered by the Red Cross Knight) who demands chivalric treatment by her male colleagues but delights in harrying freshmen and sophomores, especially the women, and is bitterly and caustically suspicious of all newcomers and young instructors.

In such a college standards are often low, and sometimes adjusted to meet the needs of children of prominent alumni. The visiting applicant should therefore beware lest he be too easily fascinated by the beauty of the campus or the geniality of his prospective chairman.

Contrariwise, there are obvious disadvantages in a vast university. The teaching faculty is enormous; and a Department of English alone may require a hundred or more instructors. Many of these are temporary or teaching fellows who remain only for a year of two, but the permanent body is more than sixty professors, associates and assistants. Large departments develop a kind of nationalistic spirit; each defines its own boundaries, lays down an iron curtain and resents invasion. Yet the adequate study of English demands a knowledge of dramatics, art, history, music, philosophy and psychology adapted for its own needs. However, this habit of rigid departmental isolation is as rampant in small colleges.

Another disadvantage is that the organization must be vast and impersonal, with a horde of administrators each with his office, secretary, notepaper, perquisites and prerogatives. Few individual faculty members know their dean, and fewer exchange even formal words with the president. And in an institution nominally democratic so many decisions have to be made that the burden of committees, and committees, and committees, is overwhelming. Fortunately, there are some men who enjoy committees.

But there are greater compensations. This vaster university world has its own microcosms of kindred enthusiasts for most things. Most departments include experts of international reputation, and within each there are half a dozen colleagues who can discuss any scholarly or critical problem with exact and specialized knowledge.

Before finally making his choice—if he is so lucky as to be able to choose—the applicant should weigh all the probabilities. Small colleges change rapidly; ultimately even the most disagreeable colleague retires and the date can be prognosticated. Contact with colleagues and with students is closer and often more rewarding; friendships are more easily made and last longer. And on the campus even the most junior instructor is an important person. In a large university the individual professor, no matter how celebrated in his own world of learning, is but one in two thousand. His students come and go, and thereafter he seldom sees or hears of them again, unless perchance one of them needs an immediate testimonial.

A first appointment should be regarded as a period of

apprenticeship; nor should the newcomer too rapidly put down deep roots. He will become the better teacher if he has achieved varied experiences of different kinds of university. In spite of the protests of his growing children, he gains in stature if he shifts his camp every ten years.

Appointments however are as much the concern of those who make them! Experienced chairmen look for certain qualities in an applicant which are not usually ascertainable from the grade records provided by the registrar of his university. Somewhere in the sheaf of glowing testimonials should occur the note "gets on well with people." Without this gift, the newcomer, in spite of his *summa cum laude* sheepskin and his Phi Beta Kappa key, can become a burden and a nuisance. Yet this ability to serve with others should not be mere placid docility. Keen and able young instructors are naturally eager reformers, and critical of their elders. A department without its own internal critics may be congenial but is seldom efficient.

Even more important, the chairman looks for signs that the newcomer will go on growing to the end. Some teachers petrify at forty; others are at their best in their seventies. The gift of growth depends on so many factors; it can be stunted by bad health, happy (or unhappy) marriage, overweening ambition, premature success and too rapid or too tardy promotion. Though it is impossible ever to predict that any individual will continue to be a good grower, the runts can usually be discerned early. Unless a man has shown sign of bearing fruit by thirty, he is not likely to achieve much in his forties; and by fifty he becomes one of those worthy colleagues who are such a nightmare to a conscientious dean—the man whom it would be brutal to eject—and wrong to promote; and who finally achieves security of tenure to end a career of blameless mediocrity. Such men form four fifths of any faculty in any university.

In present conditions in American universities, when more are demanded as teachers than the graduate schools can produce, mediocrities are no longer eliminated by competition. But even with the brutal and ferocious public competition for first and senior appointments which still exists in the English universities, where every junior vacancy is sought by forty qualified applicants, results are much the same. Few young English lecturers would admit that their seniors are invariably men of surpassing distinction in the world of letters. The truth of the matter is that greatness in teaching or in scholarship is as rare as greatness in any other calling.

Professors in the highest rank in the greater American universities are of two kinds: those who have reached the top by patient merit, and those who have been allured from other institutions. The processes leading to such an appointment are subtle and on the whole work well.

Departments of English are so large that each needs specialists for the different courses and interests. Moreover, it adds to the prestige of a university to have on its faculty men known outside for their published works and standing, and there is keen competition to secure them.

When a vacancy is foreseen, the chairman of the department looks around for a likely candidate whom he invites to visit the university either to teach in the summer semester or to give a public lecture. The visitor is treated with great hospitality. He meets the dean and the seniors of the department, and they respectfully draw out his views on professional matters. They also privately quiz his personality and social manners. Nothing direct is said or hinted on either side but all are aware of the situation. When the visitor has departed, he is anatomized by the chairman and his colleagues. If they like him, he receives a letter inquiring whether he would entertain an offer to join the department.

At this point the candidate is in an enviable position. Usually his present university will try to keep him, for it will lose face if he leaves: he is showing that in his estimation, the new is better than the old. It makes a counteroffer of increased salary and more favorable conditions of work. The candidate must then choose whether to stay where he is, with his glory enhanced, or whether to bargain for an even better offer. He may, of course, receive the snub direct from his present university; if so, he accepts the new invitation without further ado.

A rising academic is not, however, entirely at the mercy of Fate. He can court offers in various ways. Directly, or through an influential advocate, he can hint that he would welcome an invitation from the university of his choice; or he can let it be more widely known that he is unsettled and is seeking other fields. The commonest way of proclaiming that he is—to put it crudely—for hire is to read a paper at the annual meeting of the Modern Language Association, where 5,000 or more teachers of modern languages gather together in December or September. The chief function of this slave market is to enable ambitious aspirants to parade before chairmen of departments.

In English universities the situation and methods of selection are very different. "Professor" is not an academic rank but an appointment; and since there is usually but one professor in a department (of which he is the permanent head), before the Second World War there were fewer than twenty-five full professors of English in all England.

When a vacancy occurs, a notice is published in the London *Times,* setting out the salary and the terms of appointment, and inviting applications. The candidate is required to present ten to fifty copies of three testimonials and to name three other persons who will testify to his abilities. The applications —seldom less than twenty—are scrutinized, and a short list of four or five candidates is compiled. Each is then summoned to appear for interview before the board of selectors, who ask him a few perfunctory questions. In due course a decision is announced.

In theory, public advertisement attracts the best candidates, and the process of selection is judicial and objective. In practice, there is fierce underhand competition between senior professors of rival universities, each pushing his own candidate, and much private pressure on the members of the board. Since these selectors are seldom experts in the subject, and are therefore unable to judge the professional merits of the candidates, they are greatly influenced by the recommendations of their advisers. It is thus far more important for a candidate to have skillful and influential backers than an imposing list of publications or known skill in teaching or lecturing. Men from the University of Oxford are in a peculiarly strong position, for in that ancient institution the subtle art of wire-pulling is better understood than elsewhere.

This method of selection has several evil effects. Most academics below the standing of professor are inadequately paid and live in a state of genteel semipoverty; competition for Chairs is fierce and bitter. Disappointment, and especially repeated disappointment, breeds malcontents. Sometimes, when there is an even vote between two good candidates, the board compromises on a weak third. There is thus a general and cynical belief that appointments are seldom made objectively on the merits of the candidates. This feeling is strengthened when from time to time it is learned that the choice had in fact already been made (and sometimes even privately confirmed) not only before the interview but even before the vacancy was advertised. Thus jealousies and rivalries are engendered. Every college and university has its quota of middle-aged men who spend the last ten or fifteen years of their service disappointed, frustrated and embittered, snarling with Iago

Preferment goes by letter and affection,
And not by old gradation, where each second
Stood heir to the first.

In an American university any man who has shown competent zeal in teaching and publication can expect to reach the rank of professor by his middle forties. Naturally the title of "professor" is less respected than in England, but the professor himself is in smaller danger of excessive self-reverence.

A good Department of English should include a diversity of

creatures, like a good Zoo, which is incomplete without its lion, giraffe, hippopotamus and giant sloth, not omitting the indigenous fauna such as the viper and the skunk, who usually are also unbidden specimens in the collection. Personality is far more important for a teacher than an assortment of degrees and diplomas.

The Cambridge School of English, when I was a student in 1920, was rich in personalities, such as A. B. Cook (famous for a colossal work on Zeus), who lectured on the origins of Greek tragedy—folklore not literary. He had a precise manner, a well-organized and twinkling mind, and a pretty but proper wit. G. G. Coulton was the expert for "life and thought" in the Middle Ages, a peripatetic lecturer, long and thin and wild. He possessed, seemingly, vast knowledge, but presented it untidily. Coulton had several handicaps: a hatred, almost neurotic, for the Catholic church and all its works, and an aggrieved pugnacity which may have compensated for an *aegrotat* degree.

More exciting was Mansfield Forbes on "The Poetry of the Romantic Period and the Child." His course was typical of the best kind of Cambridge lecture. It was neither "survey" nor "prerequisite" nor of direct use for any examination, but the thoughts and excitements of a man fascinated by something he has discovered. Such lectures are often chapters of a book in gestation. As with others who have said good things about children, Forbes was a bachelor. He died young.

The most stimulating of all was I. A. Richards. His first course of lectures was on "The Theory of Criticism in Literature." He began by rejecting the two popular and accepted critical approaches: the "Saintsbury" critical school, with its belief that no real criticism was possible, only the expression of individual preferences; and the other theory that a specific thrill is caused by great works of art (which A. E. Housman later located in the stomach)—a doctrine held mainly by those weary of criticism, and by beginners. Then by diagram and dialectic, Richards proceeded to analyze the nature of the poetic response and the ways words function. For criticism, he claimed, we must assume a reader of normal mind, unconstrained in his emotional response, educated to appreciate what he reads. Thus the conditions for critical judgments in the "standard reader" are sanity, instruction and literary experience. All critical theories must square with a reader's experiences; there are no extraneous tests of a poem. This was the first statement which Richards afterward much elaborated.

These lectures, given to a small audience without flourish (and sometimes inaudibly), were exciting to some of us. Others found them unappetizing and disturbing; they dropped away. In succeeding years Richards' views developed as he learned by experimenting on his hearers; and in time he gathered around him a kind of school of new critics, not all of whom possessed the master's essential sanity, sense of humor, or literary experience.

Far more important than lectures was the personal direction of one's tutor. Since there was no tutor for English in my own college, I shifted for myself and had the good sense to seek help from S. C. Roberts (then an assistant secretary at the University Press, and afterward Sir Sydney Roberts, Master of Pembroke and Vice-Chancellor). The evenings I spent with him were the most useful and enduring of all my Cambridge experiences. Twice a week I wrote an essay of about 2,000 words which I would read aloud and he criticized. He taught me the elementary principles of literary writing, which are simple but usually overlooked. Read originals and not critics. Prefer particular judgments to wide generalizations. Never give a secondhand judgment. Your own judgment, however immature, is worth more than quotations from other people's. Prove all opinions by quotation and reference. It is better to have read two novels by Dickens than five books about him. All this is just common sense, but so seldom realized by most undergraduates or indeed by most writers in learned journals.

After Roberts, I tried I. A. Richards as a tutor for the poets of the romantic period. I was his first private pupil, but not (I suspect) his most prized. Essays were now concerned more with ideas and less with style and method, as we explored Shelley, Coleridge, Wordsworth and Byron. Once we fell to talking about a poet's self-revelation in his work, and he put me to construct a life of Burns from his poetry (I having at that time no knowledge of the facts). The results were not too far from the truth. Such an experiment would be a useful check on some modern critical-psychological theories of art. It would require a psychologist to study the work of a writer without any previous or outside knowledge of his life or environment. An expert so conditioned might be difficult to find; but perhaps not.

Examinations of some kind are a modern but regrettable necessity. In medieval times, a student was granted his degree when he had fulfilled his terms of residence and presented the university with testimony from his teachers that in their opinion he was worthy of the degree. In more competitive ages, a university requires some verifiable evidence of the comparative ability of its students. But the methods of winning a degree vary from place to place. At Cambridge (and I believe Oxford) the first prerequisite is known as "pernoctation": before graduating a student has to produce evidence that he has slept in college fifty-nine nights in each of nine terms. It is assumed that if he has spent his nights in college he has probably spent his days in study. Thereafter he is entitled to sit for the examination that establishes his class and standing. In the Inns of Court in London the barrister-to-be qualifies by eating a prescribed number of dinners. However, in the more prosaic University of London, students are required to have attended their classes with due regularity.

In the Cambridge system the final comprehensive examination for the B.A. was one of the great crises in a man's life, for his career would depend largely on the class he obtained. Finals are like track racing; they call for special and intensive training. In this desperate situation I devised a Five Point System, which has since benefited several of my better students.

In a comprehensive examination the victim has two kinds of problem. If he is replete with knowledge, he must have some way of extracting and arranging it on demand and almost instantaneously. If he is perilously short of information, he must know how to use every one of his few facts.

The system aims to provide a kind of mental machine which will almost mechanically extract and sort the contents of the mind. It functions thus: Suppose a problem requiring a knowledge of several authors—a discussion, for instance, concerning the Romantic Movement. Jot down the names of five major authors. For each author jot down five titles. Already we have twenty-five things to say. Every title is then considered under five heads: theme, plot (or argument, or "what it says"), character (or imagery, or peculiarities), diction (or versification, manner of writing, or "how it says it"), special qualities (or remarkable passages, quotable lines, memorable scenes). For each heading (except for theme) we can usually find five things to say; and by this time—about three minutes—we have collected about 500 illustrations! It does not always work out quite so smoothly but seldom fails to produce at least a respectable array of illustrative facts.

Having devised the system, I put myself through the drill on every likely problem and author. Suppose a question on *Othello*. Even after a first reading, it is not difficult to have some idea of the theme, plot (five major developments), characters (five major persons), diction (five important speeches), special qualities (five remarkable episodes). And for each heading five comments. Admittedly, this kind of mental process is some way removed from the higher reaches of Aristotle or T. S. Eliot; but it does galvanize a sluggish mind, and it fosters alert reading.

The system of a comprehensive examination to test a student's ability and final academic standing is not generally used in American universities. Instead, the regulations demand that all students for the degree of bachelor of arts shall endure a variety of courses which are valued in "hours." A "3 hour course" means that the student shall sit for three hours a week for a whole semester (of fifteen weeks) imbibing instruction in the classroom. When enough "hours" (usually 120), distributed according to the prescribed pattern, have been collected the student's liberal education is complete. Each course is examined at its close by the teacher, who grades his students A, B, C, D, and in extreme cases E. There is no general or final examination.

There are two reasons for this rigidity. For the convenience of registrars and such persons, all courses have the same "weight" and it is assumed that each has the same value. Thus one clock hour of instruction in Homer's *Odyssey* = one hour of Industrial Management = one hour of the Theory of Dimension = one hour of Harmony, Counterpoint and Instrumentation = one hour of Human Ecology = .002777 of a Liberal Education. The second reason is that a student need not take all his courses at the same school. If he has sat through three hours of Major Writers of the Renaissance at Puddleduck State College, he can be credited with that course at Illinois Universal.

For the study of English literature the course system can be excessive and even pernicious. Literature is to be studied chiefly by reading books, and since there are many books to be read, as few classes as possible should come between the student and the book. The good student may be expected to work on an average for forty-five hours a week, during which he takes five courses. If in each course he must spend three hours a week in the classroom, only six hours remain for reading. Moreover, excessive lecturing and teaching destroy initiative in a student, for he soon gets into the way of thinking that his work is done if he can repeat what the lecturer said.

It is disastrous also for the teacher. A straight lecture in English consists of at least 4,000 words. If he gives nine lectures a week during an academic year of thirty weeks, he will by the end have emitted well over a million words, or the length of more than twelve full-length novels. No man can maintain quality in such quantity. If lectures are stimulating, they should be taken—like other stimulants—moderately; if bad, one a week is too many.

In such a system the final examination in each course is of less importance than elsewhere. Since the instructor composes his own examination paper, there is no generally accepted standard or art of examining. Some teachers expect their students to give back what they have received; their tests seldom provoke thought or allow for disagreement.

So far as I have observed, the examinations set by some of my colleagues (even for the Ph.D. preliminary) too often encourage glib summary rather than considered answers. It is not uncommon to encounter such a question as "Discuss [in 25 minutes] the influence of Plato on English writers of the Renaissance." This kind of question can only be answered by one who has crammed his information from the suitable textbook; he has no time to pause and think. And so with other questions which demand an instantaneous display of accepted opinions. Actually, the simplest general questions are the most searching. Ask a student about the sources of *Comus* and he repeats what he remembers of the editor's introduction; ask him for his opinion of Milton, and he inevitably reveals the quality of his mind.

Teachers of English literature have their own special problems in examining and grading their students. The process must be intuitive, and therefore subjective and fallible. The student's judgment of *The Tragedy of King Lear* cannot be condensed to a series of multiple choices—"check one of the following critical pronouncements"—because there is no final "right" judgment of *Lear*.

In the course system, the main purpose of the examination is to confirm the teacher's impression of the quality of individual students as it has been revealed in their periodical essays, especially when from time to time he feels an uneasy suspicion that a brilliant essay is not necessarily the work of its putative author. In some places, especially where a professor sets the same question year after year, there is a brisk trade in old essays. Once, in a Canadian College where I taught, a student purchased an A-grade essay, presented it as his own, and to his indignant fury received it back graded D; an event which prompted several cynical observations among that professor's colleagues. But a teacher who is too idle to devise new examinations is himself largely responsible for dishonesty in his students.

Where instructor and students have established the right relationship the final examination can be a joyous experience for both parties. Questions are so devised that they give every student a chance of showing off his best qualities; and the answers reveal to the instructor what his students have learned. If the examination reveals that they have learned very little, then the course needs to be revised drastically—which is worth knowing.

In this kind of friendly examination, questions should be a challenge; that is, the student should be given problems in criticism or interpretation that have not previously occurred to him. Let him be asked to consider *dicta* which run clean contrary to everything he has been taught, such as "Give your own opinion on the following observations—'Donne's reputation is vastly overdone.' . . . 'No one would willingly read all through Joyce's *Ulysses* unless his professor demanded it.' . . . 'There is much to be said for Dr. Johnson's low opinion of *Lycidas*.'" Occasionally a student should be allowed to relieve his pressures by an open invitation to criticize his teacher. Some of the best answers I have yet read have been to the question "If there was any opinion expressed in this course with which you have particularly disagreed, state it and refute it." However, that kind of question can only be asked when the student has entire trust in his instructor's integrity; otherwise only the bravest and the brashest choose it. It demands that close sympathy in the classroom between teacher and taught which I have encountered only in American universities.

The atmosphere of the classroom depends greatly on the

tradition of the university and on the previous background of its students. In London, few professors and fewer students lived near the college or in London. Academic life was entirely separate from social, and we seldom visited each other at home. Of a morning we were sucked in by the Underground, and of an evening we were dispersed to the suburbs. Nor was there much friendly contact between faculty and students, who seldom showed any desire to get to know their teachers. Often, the common attitude was that we were paid to provide instruction to enable them to pass the examinations. So long as we gave reasonable value, no more could be expected. As a body, London students were seldom exciting. To some extent this apathy was due to their conditioning. Most of them passed from the elementary schools to the secondary with State aid. The State paid for their university education. They were preparing to become teachers in State-supported schools. They would retire on State-provided pensions. And ultimately the State would contribute to their funerals. That system does not foster any wild spirit of adventure, either of body or of mind.

It was different with those who took the M.A. or the Ph.D. Each chose a single supervisor to advise and direct his research; the relationship was that of apprentice and master, and lasting friendships often followed. When the thesis was finished, the candidate was quizzed *viva voce* by his supervisor and one other examiner; if they disagreed (which was seldom), a third examiner could be brought in to adjudicate. It could, however, sometimes happen that when the examiners were jealous rivals, one would score off the other by damning the work of his student. The standard required for theses was very high, and the results were usually real "contributions to learning." For such higher degrees there were no courses in bibliography or method; the student learned by imitation or from his master.

Such Canadian students as I encountered during six years at Queen's University in Kingston, Ontario, had their peculiar handicaps. The educational system was a compromise between the Scottish and the American. Final examinations were all-important but the teacher was also the examiner of his own course. Originally the University was a Scottish foundation and still maintained some of its rugged, at times uncouth, traditions. It was, for instance, tribal custom for students, especially in the earlier years, to have as little as possible to do with their teachers, who were to be regarded as the Enemy. The rare individual who tried to get to know his professors was despised and opprobriously labeled.

All students in arts were in theory literate; they had passed an examination in English set by the Ontario Department of Education. In the first year therefore they were herded into large classes for a compulsory survey of English literature, for which few had much zeal or ability; and they floundered through with such surreptitious aids as they could acquire. One Kingston tradesman ran a profitable racket by selling notes for the English examination; but these were so inaccurate and full of elementary errors in spelling and fact that their use was immediately obvious. Most of the freshmen were handicapped by cultural malnutrition; few had ever seen a play acted even by amateurs, fewer by professionals. They were an incalculable audience in the campus theater. Ophelia mad provoked loud mirth, and a love scene no matter how tenderly presented was often greeted with catcalls.

This boorish behavior was partly fostered by bad traditions in the high school, where an interest in drama was taken as a sign of effeminacy. From time to time high-school teachers would arrange for their students special performances of good drama which were wrecked by their derisive hostility. On one occasion students from a wide area were transported by motor coach to witness a performance of *Murder in the Cathedral,* which was inaudible because most of them brought their portable radios to listen to the hockey game. Such teen-age opposition to culture is the more surprising because in Canada the adult enthusiasm for drama and the arts is noticeably keen.

The smaller group of a dozen or a score Queen's students who took English honors in their second and third years were more rewarding; they had shaken off the crudities of their first year and became keen, friendly and sometimes very able. These experiences however are now more than twenty years old; conditions have doubtless changed, especially with the success of the annual Shakespeare Festival at Stratford, Ontario.

Students in America also have their idiosyncracies. To anyone who has endured the rather rigid English upbringing, the young American is a surprise, and often a shock. Children are seldom obedient; their parents have been so awed by the psychologists that they go about in terror of wounding the little egos of their offspring. Teen-agers, too, appear to be rude to their parents, uncontrolled and uncontrollable, prematurely oversexed, inevitable delinquents. . . . And then the miracle happens. Quite suddenly—at the age of eighteen or so—boys and girls change almost overnight as drastically as caterpillars into butterflies. They become poised, charming and delightful.

As students, however, some of them have handicaps. Their intellectual upbringing has been too orderly, too much conditioned and regimented. They expect direction. They lack independence of judgment and that first quality in a good student—insatiable curiosity. Their general knowledge is weak, and they have little care for anything but the immediate present. And too many of them are town bred and without imagination.

This lack of general knowledge is sometimes surprising even to the native-born teacher. A colleague was about to discuss Browning's "Soliloquy of the Spanish Cloister" with a group of freshmen. On inquiry he found that none knew the meaning of *soliloquy* or *cloister*. To another group the tragic ending of *Romeo and Juliet* seemed senseless. Why, one asked, couldn't Romeo get a job at a gas station? And what was to stop Juliet from hopping on a Greyhound bus and joining him at Mantua? Then she could find a job as a waitress, and they could have gotten along quite well till things were straightened out. It was a weakness in the play that this solution had not occurred to Friar Laurence or to Shakespeare. However, it may be assumed that this youth was unlikely to become an English major.

Nevertheless, of all students that I have encountered, the American are the most fascinating and rewarding to teach. They have charming manners, they are full of zest and energy, and they are entirely friendly and very frank. They thank their teachers for good teaching, and they forthrightly criticize bad. The dumb, surly or resentful student is rare.

6 ✦ *Prejudices*

Experience, says the old saw, is a great teacher; it is also a breeder of prejudices, and it is well to be aware of them. Mine include a profound respect for discipline in all its manifestations, from the ascetic life of the Carthusian and the education of members of the Society of Jesus to the close-order drill of the Brigade of Guards, and even the rhythmic prancing of the Rockettes. In modern social theory, however, discipline is seldom regarded as a cardinal virtue, for it is a manifestation of authority, and it is no longer quite nice to accept authority, immediate or ultimate, although without ultimate discipline the Great Chain of Being would be as frustrating as a tangled fishing line.

In education especially this word "discipline" has a sour sound; it smells of canes, straps, and paddles, of irregular verbs learned by heart, of soulless drudgery, and stupid sadistic teachers.

My own introduction to Shakespeare was by way of this kind of discipline. The texts assigned were edited by A. W. Verity for the Cambridge Press, scholarly works in their own way, but hardly suitable for the eager young. Verity supplied an introduction with the usual facts of date and source, and a literary section on the plot and the characters—we were commanded to learn these almost by heart, for there was sure to be a question on Rosalind's character in the ensuing school certificate examination. At the back of the book, Verity gave notes on every word and phrase which could cause any difficulty; he also added a glossary, learned and philological, on all those words that delight lexicographers, with the Greek, Latin, Anglo-Saxon, Norse, Icelandic, High German and Old French forms and the rest, with supporting quotations. The reader was directed to this glossary by "See G." in the notes; and woe to that wretched boy who overlooked "See G." Each of us in turn was called upon to expound the meaning of every line and to repeat Verity's scholarly gloss. It is a tribute to Shakespeare that I survived such methods of exposition.

In spite of its dreariness, this kind of teaching had its ultimate advantages; it bred caution in the young reader, who quickly learned that in Shakespeare things were seldom quite what they seemed. He was thus forced always to verify his references and to read carefully. I would add that all his boys had a great respect and fear for this particular master, who was one of those characters whom one always remembers with real affection.

The reaction from discipline, especially for the young, is one of several ultimate backwashes of that revolution loosely called the Renaissance. Fine word, "renaissance"; it means "rebirth." The Victorian critics who first used it in the mid-nineteenth century grew lyrical. John Addington Symonds cried out with full throat, "What the word Renaissance really means is new birth to liberty—the spirit of mankind recovering consciousness, and the power of self determination, recognising the beauty of the outer world, and of the body through art, liberating the reason in science, and the conscience through religion, restoring culture to the intelligence, and establishing the principle of political freedom." The final result of this rejection of authority was summed up in Bernard Shaw's dictum that the Golden Rule is that there is no Golden Rule. And since the rules for education can no longer be deduced from authority, educators by empiric observation have induced pedagogic chaos in the conclusion that the dear children must themselves decide what they want to learn. Once when I suggested to a gathering of teachers of English that it was good to require young students to learn poetry by heart, I was heavily rebuked for such a reactionary proposal: young students do not like being made to learn by heart. A large pile of millstones lies stacked ready for those educators who have so wronged children by refusing them the blessing of disciplined learning.

Discipline is the outward sign of authority, without which ordered existence is soon usurped by the great Anarch who rules by glibly persuading his subjects to abrogate their responsibilities. Parents surrender their natural rights and duties to teachers, who in turn lean on administrators and superintendents, who rely on theorists, who put their final trust in the *faeces* of the I.B.M. machine (as Roman augurs predetermined the future by peering into the entrails of slaughtered sheep).

The hapless child is thus deprived of his right to that definite authoritative guidance which his parents are too bewildered to give him. Subconsciously he yearns for the direct "no" and even the decisive slap. But parents never say "no"; instead they offer him, even before he can talk, arguments and reasons for his behavior which are usually unconvincing rationalizations of their own uncertainties. The child soon learns to despise such irresolution and turns for guidance to the GADARENE LAW, or the Common Will of the Gang: "Let's follow the rest of the herd," as the hindmost swine cried out to each other when their leaders began to rush down into the sea.

The greatest social need in modern education is the Community College for Fathers and Mothers, wherein they may learn elementary lessons in the art of parenthood which their parents neglected to teach them. To qualify to teach in the college instructors must have been harmoniously married to one spouse for at least fifteen years (professors for twenty-five), have brought up four or more children noted by their neighbors as sane, happy, healthy and well balanced, and be acclaimed by secret ballot of fellow citizens as Wise Parents. Courses of instruction shall be entirely practical, for parenthood is an art, not a science. No persons who are by profession industrialists, psychiatrists, sociologists, anthropologists, philosophers, educationists or academics of any kind shall be permitted to take any part in the instruction or organization of the college, or even to enter it, unless they have also acquired the highest grade as Wise Parents, when they will be eagerly welcomed. All parents of difficult, neurotic or unintegrated children will take remedial courses twice a week; and the parents of delinquents shall be compelled by severe penalties of the law to take daily courses—accompanied by their offspring. Special courses will be held for teachers who wish to restore the older kind of disciplined learning in their classrooms.

Without mental discipline, mental processes soon atrophy; the area of sensitive spots is narrowed; the personality shrivels. One of the more blatant insensitivities in so many of our college students is a lack of historical sense, or even an interest in history, which leads to the neglect by graduate students of the literature of the past. Even the best of them often prefer to write their dissertation on some modern writer or critic. Thereby they deny themselves that enriching of the personality which comes from close contact with the great minds of other generations, the effort to understand the thought and the meaning of their words, the stretching of the imagination to live in other environments. Without this experience they are incompetent to criticize even contemporary literature. An understanding of Joyce's *Ulysses* demands considerable knowledge of the literature of the past, as well as an intimate acquaintance with the doctrines, organization and liturgy of the Catholic church.

One of the first lessons which man must learn to become civilized is that the Chain of Being did not begin at the moment when his mother conceived him, and will not end at the marriage of his youngest daughter. It is too wild a dream that everyone seeking public office should demonstrate a proficient knowledge of history before he attempts to make it; but the efforts of a future teacher of English can more easily be controlled.

Elaborate criticism of modern works is, or should be, unnecessary. The writer is speaking to his own generation in their common language. If he knows how to write and they have learned to read, the meaning is clear. If he cannot communicate his meaning, he is either a bad craftsman, or a muddled thinker, or he has mistaken his medium; his broodings should rather have been expressed in music.

"But no," cries the indignant critic. "The art of writing lies not in clarity but in allusive profundity. The great writer demands that you wrestle with his meaning which is too deep, too personal for direct expression. He calls upon you to share a great mental effort. You must condition yourself to his ways, not he to yours. But, of course," the critic adds coyly, "you can hardly hope to understand him without my professional guidance."

It was (perhaps) my misfortune to have been brought up to respect Q's demand (in *The Art of Writing*) that the author owes it to his readers above all things to be clear; "the business of writing demands two—the author and the reader. Add to this what is equally obvious, that the obligation of courtesy rests first with the author, who invites the seance, and commonly charges for it. . . . To *express* ourselves is a very small part of the business: very small and almost unimportant as compared with *impressing* ourselves: the aim of the whole process being to persuade." Q, however, was an author before he became a critic.

A great writer needs no horde of critics to proffer their services like the competing guides who tout for the tourist at the entrance to Pompeii. Instead, he looks for intelligent readers with wide general knowledge and eager curiosity, for the good reader has hooks all over, like a burr. A knowledge of life is thus more important than a course in critical theory.

Excessive training in critical analysis often develops the wrong kind of sensitivity. A critic of this sort is forever projecting himself into whatever he reads; he sees symbols everywhere. On the campus of the University of Michigan stands an erection known as the Burton Memorial Tower. Ribald, Freudian-oriented youths dub it "the phallic symbol"; so 'tis to them. But the architect built the tower that way not as a temple of Priapus, but to house a set of carillons. Much of the sexual imagery which critics discover in poetry exists likewise only in their own minds. St. Paul warned Timothy to beware of teachers with itching ears; their modern descendants suffer rather from perpetual *pruritus genitalium.* A colleague lecturing on *Paradise Lost* spoke of Adam's original sin, which was the cause of the Redemption; *o felix culpa!* He was misheard by one of his graduate students, who in the subsequent examination commented earnestly on Adam's phallic culpa.

Minute examination of imagery has its proper place in literary study so long as the critic realizes that the perception of an image depends on his own sensitivity and experience, which must have coincided with the author's; and that his insensitive areas are untouched by those images which he cannot perceive. Caroline Spurgeon, who was a pioneer in this kind of study, attempted to survey Shakespeare's imagery objectively; and the result was impressive (even when unconvincing) as she deduced therefrom Shakespeare's likes and dislikes. But in spite of the vast heap of carded images collected by her assistants, she was quite unaware—and not to her discredit—of the existence of a whole range of images which are gathered in *Shakespeare's Bawdy,* and are equally significant to other critics.

More valuable was Caroline Spurgeon's discovery of what she called an "iterative imagery" in Shakespeare's greater plays —clusters of images which, as it were, gave a tone or smell to a particular play. Even here, too, the conclusion was personal. From *Macbeth* she extracted four classes of image as particularly significant. G. Wilson Knight found five—all different. There is thus an unpredictable subjectivity even in this kind of study.

Analysis and dissection teach us how things function; but the thing itself is destroyed in the process. As soon as one pulls the petals from the rose to peer at them through the microscope, the rose has ceased to be a rose. So a poem analyzed and disintegrated into its elements ceases to be a poem, for the effect of a poem is felt, and analysis destroys feeling. So also with love. There was once a young psychologist who fell in love. He was so excited by this new experience that he thought to analyze it. In three weeks there was nothing left to analyze, and the girl had fled. It was his brother who set out to write a thesis on mother love, which he proposed to measure in units of "mommets." When he began to apply the tests to his own mother, she set upon him with a broom handle. He was so bewildered by this unscientific reaction that he was never able to determine whether to rate her score as plus or minus.

Readers of poetry enjoy a kind of mystical experience. The great mystics are famed because they have the rare faculty of expressing and recording their experiences so that others can dimly perceive their intensity. Yet there have been many dumb mystics to whom as full a share of the unitive experience has been granted, like the old man who was a parishioner of the Curé of Ars. When someone asked what happened to him in the many hours which he spent in stolid contemplation of the Blessed Sacrament, he replied, "He looks at me, and I looks at Him"—which is the heart of the matter. Likewise many most sensitive readers can only say of a poem that it delights them.

They can be trained to observe something of its technique and structure, and this knowledge increases their perception and pleasure, but the final response is still in the depth, and beyond description.

This is one of the greatest difficulties of the teacher of English. How can he ever express his own delight or communicate it to his students? Herein lies the attraction of analytical criticism. It resembles scientific method; it seems so safe, so objective, and technical polyverbosity gives a great air of erudition. It is a kind of defense against that insecurity and inadequacy, which a teacher feels when he cannot convincingly justify his own preferences to others; and insecurity is the worst of emotions in any teacher. By denying subjective judgment—his own and his students'—he can confine them to what is demonstrable. In so doing he has materialized an emotional experience into a cerebral.

Another form of the same difficulty at a lower level is common. It often happens (though more often with some than with others!) that an indignant student will question the grade given to his essay. "Why do I never get an A? I took great pains. I have said everything there is to say. And yet you give me a C." There is no answer to this complaint except "In my judgment (which I cannot justify by any kind of objective means) you have written a C paper because you have a C mind." This reply, however tactfully conveyed, always maddens the inquirer and often leaves the teacher miserable and insecure.

Experience can sometimes be comforting. In the English system of final and comprehensive examinations, each student writes several papers each of which is independently read by a different examiner. It is the usual experience that for 70 per cent of the students examined, the same student receives approximately the same grade in each of his papers. When an examiner finds that his estimates of students are in general agreement with those of his colleagues, his own standards are confirmed, and he gains self-confidence thereby. The contrary experience can be very disturbing to self-confidence!

There is obvious truth in the common complaint that we live in an age which has lost the old traditions; but tradition can be revived, above all by intelligent teachers of English, though the process must necessarily be self-conscious and more drastic than courses in Great Books. It requires not only prescribed reading but some return at least to the earlier methods of education by which tradition was kept alive. Educated men of the sixteenth, seventeenth, eighteenth and early nineteenth centuries shared a common inheritance because all were trained by the same discipline and fed the same literary food. They were drilled in the techniques and devices of language, and especially in the art of translating from Latin into English, English into Latin—the best of all exercises for understanding both languages. They developed capacious memories by daily practice in learning by rote, not only grammatical rules and principles but large chunks of the classics, which were absorbed into the system and became part of their personalities. The classics were thus a common coinage for the expression and exchange of ideas; for the classic writers are great because they have perceived and expressed fundamental truths which are the same from age to age, even though new labels have been pasted on the old bottles. God has become the *Father image,* the soul is now called the *ego* (or "the dynamic unity which is the individual"), sodomy is made respectable as *homosexuality,* virtue is transformed into *inhibition,* and a chaos of color is called *symbolic art.*

All this, translated into action, means that students at each level should undergo certain disciplines which will at first come hard because their high-school training has left most of them with soft minds and weak wills. Let them learn by heart fifty lines a week; after a couple of years they are equipped with a quiver full of apt quotations. An intelligent student in Shakespeare's age kept his notebook of memorable observations; it made him responsive to taut writing and good phrasing, and encouraged him to imitate the best. A private collection of neat *dicta* sharpens the wits. Kept over the years it becomes a valuable record of the development of taste, observation and intelligence. And the collector may also include some private aphorisms and *dicta* of his own devising which are useful when he himself turns author.

As for the prescribing of books, it is better that at every stage of development all students read the same books than that each be offered a wide choice of options, for tradition rests not on diversity but on common experience. In each year all students should be given their list of ten—twenty—thirty—works to be read with such diligence and understanding that they can be discussed with intimate knowledge. Nor need these works be dissected in formal courses but, rather, privately absorbed, hard as such a method may seem. In Hardin Craig's words (in *New Lamps for Old,* p. 156) "teaching by teachers and not learning by students has come to be the established practice in American universities"—and necessarily so, when it is part of the pedagogical doctrine that nothing—not even dating and parent-management—can be learned except in a credit course.

Works so prescribed should be graduated to suit each level of comprehension: as, for freshmen Tennyson, for sophomores Browning, for juniors Donne and for seniors Eliot. And they should be discouraged from reading the new critics until they have first been enlightened by the old; and neither until they have intimate knowledge of the original.

Appreciation of literature is enhanced by good habits of writing and a precise use of words. English is a very difficult language. I have met many foreigners who learned English and spoke it well and fluently, but only three who spoke it so well that one was not immediately aware that it was not their mother tongue; one was a Czech, one a Belgian and the third a Dutch girl. With all the others, however skillfully they expressed themselves, there was always some little indication—a phrase or an idiom that was not quite right, or more commonly an intonation or an accent. In April 1940 just before the Nazis overwhelmed Holland I was in Arnheim talking in a restaurant with my Dutch host. A young woman came up uninvited and broke into our conversation; she was very curious to know what I was doing in Holland. She said that she came from Leeds, but her accent had traces of having been learned from a Cockney. Her parting words were "Give my kind regards to dear old England." I looked at my host, and we agreed that this was one of Dr. Goebbels' agents; no English girl would have used just that phrase.

English is so difficult for two reasons; it has no fixed grammar or rules, and its vocabulary is so rich in words, each with its precise meaning. For *water* alone it has *mist, drizzle, dew, rain, trickle, rivulet, brook, stream, torrent, cascade, puddle, pond, pool, lake, river, flood, sea, ocean.* No English writer need be reduced to "heap big water." Each word has its exact meaning and the student who would become a writer must first develop a sense of words precisely used. He is handicapped in this learning by three common diseases of language: *ape-talk, lily-gilding* and *polyverbosity.*

Ape-talk is the vocabulary of the Comics, which are mental pabulum for so many. *Macbeth* was once turned into a comic strip. In Shakespeare's version of the story when Lady Macbeth comes down from the chamber where Duncan lies dead and bleeding she hisses to her terrified husband

> *My hands are of your color; but I shame*
> *To wear a heart so white.*

The comic-strip version of that speech is

> *I've fixed everything.*

Lily-gilding is an occupational disease of newspapermen, especially of those who make up the headlines. When the President of the United States uses his constitutional right of vetoing a bill passed by the Senate, the process is entirely undramatic and unemotional; but the headline screams "President Spurns Senate." *Spurn* is the correct word for a fairly rare occurrence; it means "to kick out of the way contemptuously." When the President is presented with a copy of the bill which he intends to veto, it is unlikely that he throws it to the ground in a tantrum and then kicks it around his office. The headliner in his zeal for the dramatic has committed two serious offenses: he has distorted the fact, and he has misused a word; and words, being delicate living creatures, should not be misused, above all by professional word-men. As a result of this misuse, the word *spurn* loses its meaning and status, and degenerates into a mere newspaper synonym for "reject."

The third disease of language is *polyverbosity,* sometimes called gobbledygook. This is a disease of the educated, resulting from the by-products (waste products rather) of science. Scientists of all kinds need words that shall exactly represent materials, or processes, or theories. They therefore invent new words for new discoveries and needs. Sometimes the words are good, short and expressive—*volt, nylon, plastic,* or *zip.* More often they are monstrous and polysyllabic Hellenic perversions, such as *polyethylene.*

As a result of this habit it has come to be the mark of a learned person to use long and elaborate abstract terms which need first to be translated into English before a meaning can be extracted. Thus, a scholar-critic wrote a book to show that the use of religious imagery changed in the sixteenth and seventeenth centuries; the same word used by a Catholic writer before the Reformation came to mean something quite different to a Protestant reader a century later. In speaking of *Paradise Lost* he commented that "the typological patterning of the poem controls the symbol, holding it within a firmament of dogmatic reference which Milton consciously at least had long disavowed"—a clot of verbiage which means no more than that Milton's words were often Catholic in origin although his thoughts were protestant.

Polyverbosity of this kind is a common disease of seniors and young instructors, and of some professors also. It should be repressed early and sternly. Once a student can be persuaded that the best writing is usually the briefest, he soon learns to delight in clear terse statement, and that his "yes" must be "yes" and not "semantic affirmation." This delight is achieved by forcing him always to take pains to understand the literal, surface meaning of what he reads, and by demanding absolute precision when he writes.

The most effective elementary training I ever received was not from masters at school but in composing daily orders and instructions as staff captain in charge of the administration of seventy-two miscellaneous military units. It is far easier to discuss Hamlet's complexes than to write orders which ensure that five working parties from five different units arrive at the right place at the right time equipped with proper tools for the job. One soon learns that the most seemingly simple statement can bear two meanings and that when instructions are misunderstood the fault usually lies with the wording of the original order.

So too in teaching students to write, exact description of events, places and persons is often a better way of developing self-expression than the writing of critical essays about poems and short stories which they cannot understand anyway. The art of good writing is a grace not bestowed on everyone; nor, without this gift, can it be developed even in advanced courses in critical or creative writing. Sometimes it lurks in the most unexpected places. In the First World War I had the distasteful duty of censoring the letters of the men of my platoon; and I was surprised to find how often a man, seemingly inarticulate, could produce the most vivid and graphic letter, because he was writing for someone he loved. Herein lies the secret of good writing. A good writer has a sense for what interests and delights his reader not only in the matter but in the wording—which is one reason why the letters of literary men are sometimes more valuable than their public pronouncements. The student who has a friend with whom he exchanges long weekly letters thereby learns the art unconsciously. He may also be encouraged to keep a full, frank diary—and, as an act of elementary prudence, to keep it locked up.

Love is not the only incentive for good writing; there is sometimes as great a stimulus in hate. I had a student whom no encouragement could persuade to clear statement until I suggested as a topic "Portrait of the person whom I most dislike." "My headmistress," she began; and for five pages she erupted into blistering, perfectly phrased vituperation. We had struck a gusher.

Journalism—even campus journalism—in one form or another is a fine training, for the writer must produce his copy to time, of the right length and in the required style. He learns that writing is less a matter of mystic inspiration to explore his own ego than the result of daily practice. Moreover, the journalist is usually concerned with reporting or commenting upon current events; his story is provided for him. For the last 250 years most good prose writers in English have learned their craft by journalism; and in any generation the best prose is to be found in direct reports of recent happenings. This excellence is commonly overlooked by historians of literature because the events themselves soon cease to interest readers and there is no demand for the preservation of the reports. Prose writers in the Elizabethan Age were cumbersome in their expression of ideas and self-conscious in their fiction; they were unsurpassed when they had a story to tell or a gossipy letter to write; but since few of these have been reprinted, they are forgotten. Lyly, Nashe, Thomas Browne and Bacon are no more typical prose writers of their generation than James Joyce, Gertrude Stein or Virginia Woolf in the twentieth century.

In learning to write, a good student often passes through three stages. The first is the inarticulate. He has little to say and words elude him. Then suddenly he discovers the joy of playing with words as a kitten romps with a ball. His writing becomes frothy, extravagant and ridiculous. A good teacher must be alert for this development, which should be encouraged not repressed prematurely, for it is a natural stage of adolescent growth in the art. After a time exuberance subsides into controlled expression as ideas and experience mature. Shakespeare himself went through these stages from the stiffness of *Two Gentlemen of Verona* to the bubbling brilliance of *Love's Labor's Lost,* which was a necessary prelude to the perfect poise of *Twelfth Night.*

The good student should also be encouraged to enlarge his experiences. Home-keeping youth have ever homely wits. American students who normally spend the summer months working have greater opportunities of this kind than English, who must use the long vacation to catch up with the reading neglected in the distractions of the term.

The professor also should expand his own experiences in every way, above all by travel, although pilgrimages, religious and literary, have their disadvantages; they breed rackets in holy places where the local sharks batten on the inquiring stranger. Moreover, the sensitive tourist naturally shrinks from elbowing crowds that sweat through the Uffizi or St. Mark's in a hot August. If he cannot travel alone off season, he must learn to suppress the vice of snobbery and to develop the saintly art of interior recollection, for even summer travel adds infinite comprehension to his reading; he has experienced the same sights, sounds, smells and impressions as the authors whom he studies. The process takes time; for full absorption he should linger, but even a short stay gives him much.

Should the pilgrimage take him to England, then he must visit not only the usual tourist sites—Westminster Abbey, the Tower of London, the British Museum, a couple of Oxford Colleges and inevitably Stratford on Avon. He should venture farther afield: to Stonehenge, for prehistory; or Chedworth for Roman Britain; or York with its medieval houses in the Shambles, or the old glass in St. Peter's, or the great Minster, and the walls; or Chester; or Winchester and its castle, with the great Round Table (not indeed Arthur's own, but older than Malory), and its hall where Ralegh was condemned; or Durham; or Ludlow, where *Comus* was first played in the ruined great hall; or the abbey ruins of Tintern or Fountains, which show him what is meant by the "dissolution" of the monasteries; or Hampton Court which Wolsey built and Henry VIII took away from him and its hall where Shakespeare played; or the hall of the Middle Temple where *Twelfth Night* was played on February 2, 1602; or Gloucester, with its great Norman cathedral, and the tomb of Marlowe's Edward II, and the memorial window to the heroes of Crécy, and the New Inn where also Elizabethan plays were acted on an humbler scale than at the Old Vic.

And when he visits Stratford on Avon, let him go another seven miles to Warwick to see the castle, and the Abbey Church of St. Mary, where Bernard Shaw's Warwick lies under a fifteenth-century tomb surprisingly modern, and its perfect little chapter house entirely spoiled by a vast monument in the worst funereal taste of the 1620's erected to his own memory by Fulke Greville, but yet almost pardonable for its inscription—"Fulke Greville, Servant to Queen Elizabeth, Councillor to King James, Friend to Sir Philip Sidney." And if education interests him, then he should see some of the great public schools—Eton, Harrow, Winchester—and compare the Spartan squalor of their classrooms and dormitories with the newest high school in his home town; or he can see an Elizabethan schoolroom at Felsted in Essex or Shakespeare's school at Stratford on Avon. And let him visit Cambridge and pass through the old court of Queens' (unaltered since it was first built in 1448), where Erasmus taught Greek and grumbled about the beer; and the old court at Corpus where Marlowe muttered atheism; or Magdalene where Samuel Pepys' library still stands in its comely presses, arranged as he left it.

And he adds to his understanding if he visits some of the great houses—Hardwick, or Knole, or Blenheim, or even so modest an example as Loseley, where Donne's wife was brought up; and thence to Donne's morbid memorial in St. Paul's. If after Knole he goes northward to Edinburgh and to

Holyrood, the principal palace of the Scots Kings, he will realize why the Scots descended upon England with King James I like hungry hornets into a land flowing with milk and honey. And for an understanding of the eighteenth century, Bath; and thence to Brighton for the Regency, and the most extravagant of all princely follies, the Royal Pavilion. And to Hardy's country near Dorchester, over which still broods the spirit of Judge Jeffreys. And as he passes through the villages, he should always enter the village church. And he should see the Bristol Channel country—Nether Stowey and Alfoxden, where William and Dorothy and Coleridge tramped in the moonlight and begat "The Ancient Mariner" and "Peter Bell." Nor should he forget the Victorian remains, not only the vulgarities of the more opulent private houses and the pseudo-Gothic churches, but the outer ring in most towns, and —for greater understanding—some of the coal-mining towns of the Midlands.

If the pilgrim can prolong his stay in England and penetrate deeper into English life, he should get to know London, which has always been the center of English life and is disproportionately large. One seventh and more of the whole population of all England live in and around the capital, which is still the magnet for the ambitious wherever their desires lie: Parliament at Westminster for the politiques, the Bank of England and the Stock Exchange in the City for the financier, the Press in Fleet Street, the theaters round Piccadilly. Every activity has its small jostling self-perpetuating circle of "people who matter," and not least authors, critics and publishers in their dingy, inconvenient offices.

Indeed, anyone who would understand English literature must cultivate a sense for "people who matter"—sometimes called "The Establishment." They belong to no particular society (though when elderly they may be members of the Athenaeum), nor are there any asterisks to mark who's who in *Who's Who;* but anyone who reads the lives and memoirs of men of letters can hardly fail to note the same names recurring in each. A good topic for literary research would be to take a score or more names of modern authors and to discover whom each knew; the list for each would be almost the same. And all would have met in London.

Nor should he neglect good things to eat in England, for one learns about a country and its people as much through the belly as the eyes: cheese from Cheshire or Stilton or Cheddar, Melton Mowbray pork pies, York ham, jugged hare, Aylesbury duck, maids of honor from Richmond, Bath buns, Eccles cakes, cream and cider from Devon, fish fresh from the sea, salmon from the Severn, mutton from North Wales or the South Downs.

And if the Renaissance attracts him, let him then pass over to Italy and see for himself the incomparable riches that still remain after four and more centuries of systematic plunder. Then he will share the amazement of homely English travelers of the sixteenth century who had never imagined such wealth, artistic splendor or vicious sophistication, and why on their return they vaunted the variety of their experiences to the horror of Roger Ascham. Doubtless he will visit Venice and Florence and Siena and Verona, where Juliet's memory is almost as profitable as Shakespeare's. . . . And when he has entered St. Peter's in Rome let him descend into the crypt to contemplate the great bronze slab covering the mortal remains of Pope Sixtus IV with its twelve naked nymphs symbolizing the arts and sciences, of whom one only has any religious significance. She is labeled Theologia; she would as aptly have represented Pornographia. That sight too should make him thoughtful about the Renaissance.

Unless he has imbibed such experiences his knowledge of what he teaches remains one-sided and imperfect. Travel is not so necessary if his interests lie mainly in modern poets, for they are concerned less with experiences that come through the senses than with aberrations of a sophisticated mind. Here consultation with colleagues in the Departments of Neurology, Psychiatry and Sociology may be more illuminating, but if so, then the teacher of English must beware of contamination lest he confuse criticism of art with the exacter sciences, or become addicted to a technological manner of speaking which can easily infect him with the worst of professional vices—pomposity.

Pomposity is no new disease. Gratiano knew it well—

There are a sort of men whose visages
Do cream and mantle like a standing pond,
And do a willful stillness entertain,
With purpose to be dressed in an opinion
Of wisdom, gravity, profound conceit,
As who should say, 'I am Sir Oracle,
And when I ope my lips, let no dog bark!'

The "oracular approach" is another manifestation of insecurity and fear. It blankets all opposition from students, and is therefore an offense, for the aim of teaching is not to impress but to lead out; the best student is usually most critical of his teachers. A good teacher therefore encourages his students to friendly sparring, and he never claims omniscience nor hesitates to acknowledge his own ignorance; he is concerned with their growth not with his own reputation. Excessive solemnity is also a sign that the teacher takes no joy in his work, for joy is naturally expressed in laughter, which is too rare among professors of English either in the classroom or in their writings. Hilarity is perhaps inopportune in *PMLA,* but an occasional chuckle would not be amiss in a critical review.

Sooner or later every young instructor is faced with the problem of the many or the few. Is his ultimate objective to train a small elite or to attempt a mass conversion of the Philistines? Both objectives are commendable, but each needs a special technique. His task is almost impossible if he is faced by a class which contains half a dozen first-class minds, a score of plodders, and a dozen dullards. What excites the first-class mind is caviar to the dullard.

The solution of this, the greatest of problems in teaching

the humanities, is first to recognize—as so few administrators dare—that the problem exists. Great courage is required in administrators to declare boldly that students need courses designed for different capabilities; that the good student needs a minimum of class instruction and should therefore be given special treatment. Such a declaration is almost impossible in a large university, especially if supported by the State, which in theory is committed to the greatest good for the greatest number, and in practice often means the minimum of good for everyone.

In this dilemma each teacher must make his silent solitary choice. In the end he probably achieves more if he addresses himself to the few who are tuned in to his particular wave length, hoping that the rest will pick up some crumbs, or at least doze lightly. He should also realize that even with the best, each level of development needs a different treatment, and that sophomores and juniors are not yet ready for the specialties of scholarship and criticism.

The first-class student accomplishes more if relieved from formal classes of three hours a week. All he needs is a list of books and a private conference of half an hour twice monthly wherein he offers an essay that is then dissected by his teacher. From this small band of gifted students come the leaders, writers, scholars, critics and professors of the future. Ultimately they are worth more to the community than the average second-rate plodders. Mass methods of teaching are a great handicap to exceptional students. If given the special treatment which their talents deserve, most of those who finally achieve a Ph.D. would finish their university training two or three years earlier than under the present system. Sensitive appreciation of literature and an ability to diffuse it have always been rare gifts; and rarities need special handling.

7 ✦ *Shakespeare in the Classroom*

A. H. Thorndike, a considerable and much respected scholar in his day, once delivered a lecture before the British Academy wherein he declared in all seriousness (but to the amusement of that august audience) that "no American boy or girl can *escape* Shakespeare." Nor can a teacher of English. Sooner or later he finds himself in the role of puppet-master to one or more of Shakespeare's plays. His success will depend considerably on preliminary brooding and preparation.

Shakespeare can profitably be studied at several levels. The first, and for sophomores the most profitable, is to regard his plays as plays—an approach seldom favored by the hierophants. Drama is the most complex of all forms of art because it includes so many. A drama is literally a thing done, a doing or an acting, an action so presented that spectators can comprehend its meaning. The drama of *Othello* is not just the book of the words spoken but the complete presentation—actors, costumes, properties, setting, staging, movement, action and diction, all fused into a unity. Ideally, drama should be studied in the theater; but this is seldom possible, for performances of any but the most popular of Shakespeare's plays are rare on any campus. Student and teacher are thus forced to study the play from the text only, and to create the performance in their imaginations. Intelligent study, which is more than mere reading, requires also some thought for the fundamentals which apply to all drama, and concern the study of an individual play.

More than all other forms of art, drama is affected by externals, of which the crudest is that the author must satisfy his patrons or the theater is empty and the actors starve. This elementary economic fact applies to *Hamlet* as to the latest failure on Broadway. Novelist and poet can wait for the recognition of posterity; a dramatist must succeed at once. He needs a keen sense of the limitations of his medium and of the tastes of his audience.

Six main externals control the writing of a play. The first is the stage. Drama has been written for many kinds of stage. Sophocles wrote for a long narrow stage, almost surrounded by an arc of tiered seats occupied by 15,000 spectators. The pace therefore of *Antigone* was necessarily slow and dignified. Actors were hampered by masks, buskins and clinging robes. Speech was more important than action, which was hardly possible. Moreover, the last spectator was a hundred yards away from the center of the stage. Shakespeare wrote for a small and intimate theater; his actors were less than seventy feet away from the farthest spectator.

The second is the manner of presentation. Greek tragedies were highly symbolic—passion plays or moralities almost. There was no attempt at realism in the acting, nor could there be when an actor was enclosed, as elaborately as a spaceman, in his mask and costume. Elizabethan drama was partly realistic, partly make-believe for an audience taught to use its imagination and to eke out the play's imperfections with its thought; but which also enjoyed crude realism.

The third is the accepted manner of acting which alters from time to time and place to place. A Greek actor needed a fine voice and little else. Elizabethan acting was noisy, lively, emotional; we would probably have regarded even the acting of Burbage—in spite of Hamlet's warning—as "ham"; but he and his audience were connoisseurs of the spoken word. They loved witty repartee and long poetic speech.

The fourth factor is the audience for whom the play is presented. Shakespeare was lucky with the audience which filled his theater; it was neither the intellectual and upper-class audience which patronized the Boy Companies, nor the tradesmen and apprentices who crowded the Rose Theater, but a compound of both. His spectators, being mixed in their tastes and perceptions, Shakespeare had to appeal to all levels of appreciation. When his company acquired the fashionable Blackfriars, their plays degenerated into highbrow drama.

The fifth is the occasion—or why the play is being acted. In Athens, tragedies were given in honor of the god Dionysus; the atmosphere was religious, though not necessarily sanctimonious. In London, Elizabethan actors played for money, as today; and a working dramatist needed to develop a quick sense for the interest and the mood of the moment.

The sixth is the financing of playing. Although far removed from the higher thoughts of most critics, finance is the most important factor in the history and development of drama. When the theater is prospering, its owners can be generous in production and bold in experiment. If the takings of *The Ten Commandments* are likely to exceed $15,000,000, Moses can be accompanied into the desert with a sizable selection of Israelites. If the total possible profit on a play is $150, cast and production must be modest; not more than six soldiers were available for *Henry V*.

Such matters are all external. They do not affect the emotional or aesthetic experience of reading the play, but they become important when a play is studied in its original setting or in the development of the art of drama; and to some extent also they may at any time concern critical judgment. When the critic is prompted to brood over the significance of some speech or scene, the answer may often lie on the surface: "the actors demanded it." It is no far-fetched guess that Shakespeare brought Osric into the fifth act of *Hamlet* because one of his fellows was a sure success with Braggart Gentleman parts; or that he wrote the passage between Jaques and Touchstone on the "quarrel on the Seventh Cause" to give Ganymede time to change her costume into Rosalind. And so with many passages, long and short, especially those of topical significance: often they have little importance in the plot (or the "total emotional impact") but they certainly kept the audience alert.

Apart from the externals, certain internal factors are common to every play. The length is limited, because of the limitations of the human anatomy. A spectator can sit for about two hours on a hard stone or wooden bench, and for three hours in an easy stall; thereafter he begins to fidget. Hence two and a half hours is the limit for a play, or, at a normal rate of speaking, about 16,000 to 20,000 words; within that short limit the author must begin and end his play. Drama is thus a most concentrated form of literary art, and because concentrated so effective.

The dramatist is limited also by the number of actors available, the size of the stage, and the taste of the audience, which is constantly changing. Modern taste is against plays in verse; attendance at *The Lady's Not for Burning* or *Murder in the Cathedral* is still regarded as somewhat of a pious exercise. Verse was usual for serious drama until the end of the eighteenth century. But in every generation the purpose of playing is the same—to move spectators in the way desired by the dramatist.

Sophomores, I have found, being unsophisticated are usually quite fascinated by such elementary considerations. They are interested also in the elements necessary in the making of a play: theme first. Theme is that brief summary which can be expressed in one sentence or even in the title—*A Winter's Tale* or *A Midsummer Night's Dream,* for instance. The theme of *Othello* is the overwhelming power of evil in a warped mind, illustrated in the story of how Iago (whom everyone supposed to be honest) poisoned Othello's mind until he brought the whole world down upon his own head. Many dramatists begin with the theme and then invent the illustration. Shakespeare seldom worked that way. Rather, he chose the story and therein found the theme, which thus became his intention in writing the play.

And here we encounter the first of the Fashionable Fallacies. "There is a maxim," says G. Wilson Knight, "that a work of art should be criticized according to the artist's 'intentions': than which no maxim could be more false. The intentions of the artist are but clouded forms which, if he attempt to crystallise them in consciousness, may prefigure a quite different reality from that which eventually emerges in his work,

> not answering the aim,
> And that unbodied figure of a thought
> That gave't shape."

But Knight is not entirely consistent, for a little later he adds, "It is therefore reasonable to conclude that the poet has chosen a series of tales to whose life-rhythm he is spontaneously attracted, and has developed them in each instance according to his vision." The distinction between "intention" and "choice" is somewhat subtle. Shakespeare's choice arose out of his intention to express his vision, and Wilson Knight's "interpretations" are in fact his notion of what Shakespeare was trying to say, that is, of his intentions.

The theme of the play is worked out in the plot, which was the Elizabethan word for plan. The plot of *Lear* is not the story of the old king who had two wicked and one good daughter and what ultimately happened, but the actual arrangement of the details of that story for stage presentation, which requires far more skill than the planning of a novel, because the play must be entirely comprehensible to an audience (usually rather simple-minded) at every moment. Shakespeare's plots, except for the few failures, are so subtle that their artistry is seldom noticed or appreciated.

Thus, as the spectator sees it for the first time, *Othello* opens with the entry of two men; our eyes tell us that one is a stocky military Master Sergeant type and the other a foolish gentleman. These facts are shown by their costume and general manner of bearing and speech. Both are highly agitated. The foolish gentleman has a grievance against his companion—

> *Tush, never tell me. I take it much unkindly*
> *That thou, Iago, who hast had my purse*
> *As if the strings were thine, shouldst know of this.*

So, we learn, the military man is called Iago. He brushes off the accusation lightly and cynically, and we immediately suspect that he is probably something of a crook. But he has his own grievances too bitter to be suppressed. He has been passed over for promotion in favor of one Michael Cassio, a Florentine, by his commander, who is a Moor. He has no cause to love the Moor. He's not one of those faithful hacks who serve their masters till they are worn out—and then cashiered. No: he looks after himself on all occasions,

> *For, sir,*
> *It is as sure as you are Roderigo,*
> *Were I the Moor, I would not be Iago.*
> *In following him, I follow but myself.*

So the foolish gentleman's name is Roderigo; and now we know just how these two stand toward each other.

To appreciate the full subtle interrelation of these two—dupe and crook—we need to see them together, if not visibly to the eye at least vividly in the imagination. "But no," says the modern critic. "Shakespeare's plays are dramatic poems; it is the words which matter." Or in L. C. Knights' words, "The only profitable approach to Shakespeare is a consideration of his plays as dramatic poems, of his use of language to obtain a total complex emotional response." To be fair, Knights did later admit that other approaches were possible.

This is the second Fashionable Fallacy. *Othello* is not a poem, nor a dramatic poem, but a drama; and the difference between the three kinds is that a poem is a verbal composition for one voice, a dramatic poem for more than one voice, while a drama is intended to be visibly acted by more than one actor; that is, in drama the experience comes to the spectator through the eyes as well as the ears—or, if the neo-critical jargon is preferred—"the spectator-perception of the totality of the dramatic complex is primarily audio-visual."

As soon as an actor appears on the stage to impersonate a speaker, he shows by his gestures, tone, manner of speaking, make-up, costume, the nature—that is, the character—of the person whom he represents.

The third Fashionable Fallacy is to deny the importance of character and its study in the critical examination of a play, for, according to this critical theory, Shakespeare's plays are not about people who love, hate, destroy each other, but "expanded metaphors" for some vast ethical homily or parable. . . .

"Two tickets, please, for Laurence Olivier's expansion of the Coriolanus metaphor. . . ."

Actors, however, are not concerned with expanding metaphors but with imitating (in the full Aristotelian sense) living persons, and their whole art is to persuade us that we are witnessing not Maurice Evans in a picturesque costume but the actions, thoughts and sufferings of Prince Hamlet; and the more successfully they force us to accept that illusion, the deeper the emotional effect of the drama. When watching a play well acted, we seldom remember the critics; we are caught up in what we see; our critical faculties are numbed.

Reading a play demands a greater effort of the imagination, for we must ourselves be director and the full cast of our unseen performance. We need not necessarily visualize minutest physical details; it is unimportant whether Roderigo wears a green or an orange doublet, or whether Desdemona's hair is blonde or brunette; but we must catch every nuance and tone of each speech. The final unheard performance is often more satisfying than reality, too often marred because the actors, especially of the minor parts, seldom understand the full meaning of their lines; and with Shakespeare at his maturest this is disastrous, for there is a significance in every word, phrase, rhythm and tone. For so fine a play as *Othello,* Pope was not being overenthusiastic when he claimed that "had all the speeches been printed without the very names of the persons, I believe one might have applied them with certainty to every speaker."

Even so early in the tragedy, diction has shown the contrast between Roderigo, with his plaintive whine, and Iago, angry and vituperative, spitting out his bitter sentences. The essential coarseness of the man is further revealed as he cries out his warning to Brabantio in such gross terms.

Not only is the closest attention to character necessary in understanding a play, it is by character that Shakespeare achieves his final effect on his audience. We become aware of Othello as a man of dignified self-possession, as a tender loving husband, then as a general who takes full command of every military situation; and we watch the change as Iago's poison affects him first with bewilderment, then with the madness of a savage, and finally, the recovery of the first dignity, now enhanced, before the end. Unless we are convinced that this Othello is a man and not a symbol, we remain unmoved; for a symbolic figure is simply a concept of the intellect.

It is most important that our sophomore should be taught to observe closely the revelation of character and motive. In so doing he is forced to get inside the *persona,* to speak his words with his emphasis, to feel as he feels. In this way his imagination is exercised and his sensitivity expanded. He should also be encouraged to bring his own experiences of life to the interpretation of the play. Even by nineteen he will have known at first hand some of the emotions suffered by the chief characters. An adolescent, especially in a mixed high school, encounters jealousy quite early, and he is lucky if he has not already suffered, with Iago, at being overpassed by a despised rival, if only for the basketball team.

As the reading proceeds—and if the instructor is a poor reader he should use one of the many phonograph recordings easily available—from time to time a pause should be made to consider the actual writing of the dialogue and its sheer verbal texture, for the art of *Othello* is subtle. Each speech is invested with its own appropriate rhythms; each scene is written with overtones and variations. The Council Scene, for example, opens with the Duke and certain Senators in earnest and anxious comparison of the latest reports from Cyprus, twice interrupted by fresh news. Their discussion is ended by the arrival of Brabantio, Othello and their followers, among them Iago and Roderigo. Brabantio intrudes his private grief and the Duke calls upon Othello to answer the old man's wild charges of witchcraft.

Thus encouraged, Othello utters a long solo—an aria almost—wherein he narrates his own history and the story of his courtship. The speech can be compared with other speeches which give explanations needed to understand the event. Explanation of this kind is necessary but often tedious and artificially inserted. Here the speech is perfectly appropriate to situation and speaker, and subtly reveals two characters—Othello's and Desdemona's—the simple-minded victim and the sophisticated young woman who knows just the right technique to allure him. Later we revise that estimate, but the first impression is confirmed by Desdemona's entire self-possession before her bewildered father and even the Duke himself. Brabantio is thus shamed before his peers, and the Duke tries to console him with some commonplace platitudes in rhymed verse, to which Brabantio retorts bitterly.

To break this distressing tension, the Duke then turns to the business of the State; rhymed verse is succeeded abruptly by terse businesslike prose. Othello accepts his commission; Desdemona asks leave to accompany her husband; the meeting breaks up. Brabantio as he passes by his new son-in-law utters a curt farewell, a gnomic, oracular couplet, which is both warning and curse:

Look to her, Moor, if thou hast eyes to see;
She has deceived her father and may thee.

Othello and Desdemona follow; Iago and Roderigo remain.

One of the greatest disadvantages in reading a play is that we are seldom able to visualize any but the speakers of the moment. We had forgotten that Iago is present. So far he has said nothing; he has observed and heard everything. On the stage we shall have been closely watching his reactions to every speech.

Blank verse now changes to a quick prose as Iago, outwardly cynical and worldly wise, comforts his dupe. Then, left alone, his utterance changes to bitter passion in blank verse—its proper medium—as he gropes for some means of satisfying his hate for Othello.

In this brief analysis, matters of staging have been ignored. However, sophomores find it helpful to consider a play in terms of the stage for which it was written. Experts may wrangle about the details and measurements of the Globe Theatre, but in general they agree that its stage was wide and flanked by two main entrances through doors at either side, and that there were two pillars (very useful for a variety of purposes) holding up a roof or canopy over the main stage, and an inner stage (whether large and permanent, or small and temporary between poles and curtains, it skills not). In writing a play the dramatist must think not only of the ethical overtones but of the practical business of where to locate a scene or by which door to remove a character.

The second act of *Othello* offers few problems in stagecraft but enough to make worth considering such matters as location, entrances and exits. The act begins with Montano and gentlemen of Cyprus appearing on the stage by one of the main doors. Cassio's ship is hailed, and soon he himself is on shore and on stage by the other main door. Thus one side of the stage (as in the Athenian theater) stands for entrances from the island, the other from the harbor. Next, from the harbor entrance, appear Desdemona, Emilia, Iago and the inevitable Roderigo; and finally Othello. Husband and wife go in, presumably through the curtains at the black of the stage, which thus becomes, as it were, Desdemona's "domestic area." Iago advises Roderigo, and both go out together by the island exit. Then the herald is given his brief scene, either center stage or aloft.

At II.3, Othello and Desdemona emerge from the center—it will usually be found that characters reappear whence they last made their exit. Othello gives his orders for the night guard to Cassio, and he goes back with Desdemona to their wedding night. Iago enters from the island entrance, followed by the Cyprus gallants, and finally Roderigo appears. Cassio chases him away by the harbor entrance and then returns. The fight with Montano follows, and Othello suddenly reappears from behind and quells the brawl. A few moments later Desdemona also appears through the back curtains. Othello leads her in; the wounded Montano is carried through the island entrance; and once more Iago and Roderigo are together.

Later scenes and episodes provoke greater arguments. Where and how did Othello hide to overhear Iago question Cassio about Bianca? Does he stand in front of one of the pillars while they converse at the rear of the stage? Or is he at the rear of the stage? or at the side? or aloft? And was the scene where Othello pretends that Desdemona is a harlot acted on the upper stage, or the inner stage, or front stage? And where was IV.3—the scene where Desdemona undresses for bed—played? Or what is the "bulk" behind which Roderigo stands to waylay Cassio in V.1? And where does Othello listen when Cassio is stabbed? on the balcony above, or at the rear of the stage? And finally where was Desdemona's bed set up? There are several problems in this last scene. How was the bed introduced? was it indeed carried on by stagehands in full sight of the audience (with Desdemona already asleep)? or was a curtain pulled aside on the inner stage? or aloft? And at the end of the play when Desdemona lies dead in her bed with Othello beside her, and Emilia also dead on the ground, how were the bodies disposed of? There is no general stage curtain and no direction for the removal of the dead. How were they finally carried away or hidden?

By this kind of demonstration the sophomore learns to see *Othello* as a drama, as an imitation of human suffering and emotion, as an example of superb literary technique, as the work of an expert in stagecraft with a great sense of the theater. Probably he misses much: the iterative imagery, the ethical overtones, the complex cosmic patterns. No matter; he is not yet ready for these higher considerations. When—but not before—he has come to know the play intimately, he can profitably be introduced to the critics of the older school, of whom A. C. Bradley is the first. If not already inoculated with neo-critical notions, sophomores find *Shakespearean Tragedy* exciting; they catch the same kind of thrill as Miranda when first she set eyes on Ferdinand. And Bradley's lectures on *Othello* are his best.

There are serious objections to Bradley's minute analyses of the play. He was unduly puzzled by some of its minor inconsistencies, not always realizing that Shakespeare could be careless with minute details, or, rather, that he ignored them, for his concern was with the effect of the scene as it is being played, and not that some remark in the last act should necessarily tally with what had been said in the first.

After Bradley, Harley Granville-Barker's *Preface to Othello*. Granville-Barker combined a keen critical sense with the practical experience of one who had been actor, director and playwright. His *Othello* is not the best of his *Prefaces;* when it was written, Granville-Barker had long left the theater and was degenerating into a professor and critic. All the same, it is a stimulating companion and corrective to *Shakespearean Tragedy,* for which he had the greatest respect.

So far the sophomore has neglected serious historical and literary scholarship and textual study, except for such information as he may have gathered from what the editor offers in his textbook. Scholarship of this kind is best deferred until his fourth year or even later; and then pursued seriously. Let him now read the story as given by Cinthio, and—unaided—work out the differences between story and play. Other clues can be followed; they are given in E. K. Chambers' *William Shakespeare: A Study of Facts and Problems* and in later listings of modern scholarship.

If textual study draws him, he must first have some notion of its aims and methods. Then, before he studies W. W. Greg's opus—*The Shakespeare First Folio*—he should by himself collate a facsimile of the first quarto of *Othello* (which he can easily obtain in a Xerox copy) with a facsimile of the First Folio text. This order of study is essential. If he reads Greg or any other of the experts before he is familiar with the actual texts, either his judgment will be biased, or—more likely—he finds the intricate comparisons of reading and variants meaningless and depressing. No kind of study is less rewarding than textual scholarship at second hand. Contrariwise, a close collation of the *Othello* texts reveals why textual experts can become so excited by their differences. Whether he ultimately joins the hunt or not, he will surely realize that for the scholarly study of Shakespeare, the original text is to be preferred above all others. When this truth has been absorbed, he is ready to face modern critics; but first he needs a course in semantics to understand their vocabulary.

Shakespeare's imagery as displayed in *Othello* will probably be his first concern as he enters upon the Higher Criticism. Caroline Spurgeon (in *Shakespeare's Imagery*) tells him that the main images are of animals preying upon each other and mostly unpleasant; with a second current of sea images. More elaborate is Wolfgang Clemen's study in *The Development of Shakespeare's Imagery*—a valuable work because Clemen keeps within the bounds of common sense, realizing that even the predominant images are but a minute fragment of the whole, notes played by but one instrument in a large orchestra. From Clemen to G. Wilson Knight: "The Othello Music" in *The Wheel of Fire,* as an example of interpretation which verges on mystical vision. And so to R. B. Heilman—*Magic in the Web*—which sets out to separate all the strands in the fabric of *Othello. Magic in the Web* also serves as a countercheck to the first kind of interpretation suggested in this chapter (which Heilman labels the Fallacy of the First Night!), for poetic drama "looks both toward the theater and toward the study or library." If still unsatisfied, the graduate student can turn to Heilman's notes which direct him to the vast best of *Othello* studies.

The study of Shakespeare, as of all literature, cannot be an orderly progress. Like the squirrel sniffing over the earth for seeds, the student passes hither and thither as the scent leads him in ever-widening circles. From time to time he should test the value of all these studies, thrusting into the subsoil all knowledge and insight accumulated from scholars and critics, and returning to a straight reading—or, preferably, a good performance—of *Othello.* Dizzy raptures of the first reading can never be wholly recaptured, but for such loss there is abundant recompence. If his studies have been of any value, the play now moves him in new and deeper ways, with a sense of something far more deeply interfused, and far beyond communication in words. This is the ultimate justification of all scholarly and critical endeavor, which otherwise is but straw.

8 ✦ *The Questions Answered*

Teaching and study are one activity: we learn to teach and in teaching we learn. But in the study of literature there are two opposing creeds. Many modern critics condemn the fundamental belief of older writers—Philip Sidney, Samuel Johnson and Matthew Arnold among them—who held that literature has a profound application to life, as if, seemingly, books were written or read mainly to advance moral perfection. In this matter the teacher of English literature must adhere openly to one creed or the other, and decide whether his study is of supremest importance for right living, or whether he regards any individual work of literary art as just a specimen to be analyzed objectively into its elements of pattern, structure, metrics, image, symbol, myth and the rest; if so, he is little more than a laboratory demonstrator.

But the notion that literary art has its moral purpose can

easily be misunderstood and degraded. Great works are not cautionary tales; nor did Shakespeare write *Macbeth* as a warning against unrestrained ambition, regicide, murder, and the danger of uxorious subservience to a dominating wife; nor did he write it to fill empty urns with iterative images of clothing, bloody breeches or naked babes. Yet any sensitive reader of *Macbeth* is aware of the naked babe, and subconsciously he absorbs the moral truth that if he follows Macbeth's example he too will suffer manifold inconveniences.

Indeed, the study of literature has inevitable moral results; nor can any writer, even of drugstore shiny backs, avoid being also a teacher. This truth, so unpalatable to some, is well put by Gilbert Highet in *The Art of Teaching.* Every artist, says Highet, knows in his heart that he is saying something to the public even though the message of much modern art may sometimes be hard to define.

"In books," he continues, "the problem is much easier. Books are about people. People act in a moral world. As we read the books, we hear the voices of the characters, and see their actions. Behind both we hear the voice of the author himself implying praise of this action, making fun of that, omitting a cruel consequence here, inserting a detailed description there. All this adds up to a series of judgments about life which he wishes us to accept. Any author who heard a stranger praise his latest book by saying: 'It was beautifully written, and admirably constructed, although the way he made the characters behave was quite unreal and their standards were ridiculous,' would be deeply wounded, because it would mean that his judgments about life were rejected and nothing was praised but the pattern they made. Yet many writers will not admit this. They will not say they are trying to persuade us. They will not say they are teaching. They say: 'I am trying to put down the truth as I see it,' and if we ask: 'Why?' they shrink from the obvious answer, which is 'To communicate my view of the truth to others' and means 'To teach them what I believe.' All books contain persuasion. All books communicate a selection of judgments about life. All books try to teach. The differences are between those which teach well and those which teach badly, and between those which teach valuable things and those which teach bad or trivial things. Criticism deals with these important differences."

Even more pertinent is T. S. Eliot's essay "Religion and Literature" in which he claims that literary criticism should be completed by criticism from a definite ethical and theological standpoint, above all in fiction. "The fiction that we read affects our behaviour towards our fellow men, affects our patterns of ourselves. When we read of human beings behaving in certain ways, with the approval of the author, who gives his benediction to this behaviour by his attitude toward the result of the behaviour arranged by himself, we can be influenced towards behaving in the same way." But the whole essay should be carefully pondered by anyone who dares teach literature.

Thus the teacher-student—whom for present purposes we call the humanist—is concerned with the study of truth as expressed in literature. And back comes the echo: " 'What is Truth,' said jesting Pilate; and would not stay for an answer."

In this dilemma once more we turn to the dictionary makers for a definition of *truth.* They walk delicately and define diffusively. Thus *The Shorter Oxford:* "the quality of being true . . . to a person, principle, cause, etc. . . . honesty, uprightness, virtue, integrity . . . conformity with fact . . . absence of deceit . . . accuracy, correctness . . . true account, that which is in accordance with the fact . . . true religious belief . . . that which is true (in a general or abstract sense), reality . . . spiritual reality as the subject of revelation or object of faith . . . the fact or facts . . . the actual state of the case . . ." These are but a selection of the definitions, from which it would seem that Pilate was not jesting but as bewildered as the lexicographers.

These definitions reveal two kinds of truth: spiritual and material. Each needs different methods of inquiry and demonstration. The humanist is concerned with spiritual truth, the scientist with material. Material truth is of the surface; spiritual truth lies in the depth, with a considerable mixture of material and spiritual in the subsoil.

Literature is a record of human experience in all its variety at all levels and depths, poetry being largely concerned with the subsoil and the depths. Herein its practice and study differ from the material sciences. The physicist, the biologist and the chemist are concerned with material truth. As soon as they pursue their phenomena into the subsoil, physical becomes metaphysical, and they cease to be pure scientists, for ultimately the scientist is concerned only with that which can be weighed, measured and described. There is no disagreement or difficulty between the humanist and the scientist so long as each recognizes the validity of the other's values, for each is seeking truth in and on a different level.

Disagreement arises most acutely in those studies which concern the subsoil, such as psychology, social science, anthropology, whenever the practitioners apply the methods of science to that which is no longer solely material, and reach conclusions which cannot be verified scientifically. Herein the ultimate conflict lies between those who regard man simply as an animal with conditionable reflexes and those who regard him as having a soul.

While the true scientist must be entirely objective in his search for truth, the humanist is necessarily subjective, because truths which lie in the depths can only be apprehended intuitively. John Donne knew this well, and in "The Extasie" he expressed supremely that mingling when two souls, interinanimated by love, fuse into perfect mutual comprehension in an ecstasy so intense that it unperplexes. Only a hearer also refined by love can understand this soul's language in the depths of his own soul; but he cannot record it to be played back by a tape recorder.

This kind of intuition is quite common, at its deepest in the unitive experience of Vaughan, who saw Eternity the other night, nearer the surface in Wordsworth's perception of a presence whose dwelling is the light of setting suns and in the mind of man. To deny the validity of such experience is to fall into that negative superstition sometimes called materialism.

Some modern intellectuals are very contemptuous of the older superstitions—uncritical credulity in the interpretation of phenomena without scientific controls, excessive veneration of things and formulae, too great reliance on authority—but they have their own credulities which are far more deadly when accepted as scientific truth. The most dangerous of all modern superstitions is the belief that everything can be measured by the standard of one's own science.

This ancient fallacy Bacon labelled "Idols of the Theatre." "Lastly, there are Idols which have immigrated into men's minds from the various dogmas of philosophies, and also from wrong laws of demonstration. These I call Idols of the Theatre, because in my judgment all the received systems are but so many stage-plays, representing worlds of their own creation after an unreal and scenic fashion. Nor is it only of the systems now in vogue, or only of the ancient sects and philosophies, that I speak; for many more plays of the same kind may yet be composed and in like artificial manner set forth, seeing that errors the most widely different have nevertheless causes for the most part alike. Neither again do I mean this only of entire systems, but also of many principles and axioms in science which by tradition, credulity and negligence have come to be received."

Academic persons should always, as an act of courtesy and humility, refrain from passing judgment on their colleagues in other disciplines—until their own is invaded. The study of English literature and the Department of English are natural hunting grounds for social scientists and psychologists. Thus, for an example, a certain psychologist set out to explore the personality of Shakespeare. Since his approach was "scientific," some objective and quantitative method of measurement had to be devised. Accordingly, the number of lines assigned to each of the twelve most important characters in each play was counted, and the result was a comparative table of "character weights" or a "quantitative analysis." The basic assumption was that the top-ranking character (assigned 100 points) was the one who dominated Shakespeare's own thoughts, while the others occupied him in various degrees, so that the "ordered arrangement" revealed the "ordered structure" of Shakespeare's personality.

The tables produced some curious results. In *Hamlet,* Hamlet himself naturally scored 100 points, Claudius 39, Polonius 23, Ophelia 12, Gertrude 11; in *Coriolanus,* Coriolanus topped with 100, Menenius got 70, and Volumnia 34; in *Lear,* Lear scored 100, while Cordelia came in eleventh with a score of 15 points, while Gentleman got 13. Thus it is apparently revealed that Gertrude and Ophelia are of less importance than Polonius in the tragedy of *Hamlet;* that Volumnia is far less important than Menenius in *Coriolanus;* and that Cordelia is of so little importance in the tragedy of *Lear* that she ranks well below Cornwall and only two points above Gentleman.

When the humanist is confronted with such clotted nonsense in his own discipline, he wonders sometimes whether the same methods are applied to other studies; and his bowels are filled with chilly apprehensions when he remembers that our destinies are now in the hands of the psychologists and the social scientists. As he lies awake at the Devil's hour of three in the morning, he is haunted by the thought that the most dogma-bound communist is less threatening to personal liberty than some of his colleagues who pursue their studies on the floor above. At such moments he sees himself as a kind of deserted Elijah, harassed on all sides by the prophets of Baal, but without any hope of Elijah's drastic retaliation.

The humanist who is concerned with truths of the depths is a lonely soul. He cannot rely on tabulated experiments, true/false tests, averages, patterns of behavior or other illusory and external supports. He can proceed only by aphorism, "that hath ever some good quantity of observation," to record his own intuitions. And he needs also to have studied philosophy.

There is thus no single, comprehensive or obvious answer to our original questions. Nevertheless, in the depths we may perhaps send short signals to each other, which will convey truth, so long as we remember that the humanist is the servant of the Princess Sapientia to whom Lady Scientia is not an equal but a lady-in-waiting.

In whatever he teaches—even in Freshman Composition—the ultimate end of the humanist is to reveal to his students that the three levels—surface, subsoil, depth—apply not only to literature but also to life, for the man who has no perception of anything beneath the surface is no more than an animal. Humane studies are not only valuable but essential for right and intelligent living, and of all these studies poetry is the most universally revealing. But the ultimate communication between the poet and his readers is personal and individual; there is no agreed or final meaning in any poem, or in any other work of art. The teacher himself, unless he stagnates and breeds reptiles of the mind, also changes. Works which in one year seem trifling take on fresh and often contrary meanings; works which now appear universal fade and lose their colors. The reader receives but as he gives. Unless he has gone the same way as the writer, he misses the full meaning. When he brings new experience to his reading, the poem gives him back new significance.

Max Plowman, an intelligent critic, once told me that he never fully understood the meaning of *Hamlet* until he himself lost an only son and also had known a woman who doted on her husband yet remarried within a few weeks of his death. He had indeed realized, as an intellectual concept, Hamlet's love for his father and his disgust at his mother's remarriage; now he had experienced the like sufferings in his own soul.

This process is continually happening to the sensitive reader. At first he absorbs the poet's experience at second hand; when he himself meets the like experience, he is doubly enriched. He understands the experience, and the poem itself has become deeper and charged with new meaning.

The teacher of English is thus a light-bringer and a steward of mysteries. He cannot give his student direct experience; only life gives that; but from his own experience he illuminates. And the fuller and wider his experience, the brighter the light. But to be a light-bringer he needs first what Walter Bagehot called an experiencing nature, a mind which perceives, stores, connects everything that enters into it, which is always alive and vital. Perception is the first gift to be sought.

He needs also scholarship and critical ability. Unless he has learned the discipline of scholarship he is inexpert in exact observation, even in the precise meaning of words, without which he cannot fully understand what he is reading. The unscholarly critic as he rereads *Macbeth* may grow ecstatic at the significance of the English King who with his heavenly touch heals strangely visited people, until the earthbound scholar reminds him that Shakespeare inserted that passage as a piece of fulsome flattery for King James the First for whom a similar gift was claimed by court sycophants. Scholarly awareness is as important as critical perception but neither gift need necessarily be demonstrated by articles in *PMLA*.

Whether he publishes or not, the teacher should have his own private specializations, intimate friendships, as it were, with a few chosen authors whom he gets to know as closely as his own family. If he chooses wisely, they enlarge and enrich his personality. If he prefers one of the more strident writers—God's little apes—who scream at the world from the ample lap of a protective wife or mother, he profits less, however much he may learn of the human psyche by lifting the cover of the sewer to peer into the murky stream of consciousness. Nor need he encourage his sophomores to share in his cloacal observations, which are better postponed for maturer minds.

He learns much also from the critics of all ages, from the appreciations of the earlier enthusiasts to the close dissections of the newer generation, so long as he keeps his integrity, never approaching any critic until he has already read and made his own judgments—the earliest lesson to be impressed on his students.

He learns even more if he has a knowledge of life. Much criticism is lopsided because the critic is ignorant of the elementary facts. A learned scholar once wrote a book about Shakespeare's tragic heroes to demonstrate that Shakespeare incorporated into his tragedies the prevailing ideas of the humanists in regard to passion. Thus Othello's jealousy was illustrated from *The French Academie, The Microcosm of the World, The Blazon of Jealousie* and *The Optic Glass of Humours. Lear* was a tragedy of wrath in old age, illustrated from William Baldwin's *A Treatise of Morall Philosophie,* the *Parson's Tale,* Thomas Adams' *Diseases of the Soul,* Plutarch, John Downame's *Spiritual Physicke* and Seneca. Shakespeare may perhaps have collected his knowledge of the passions from such reading; but a directer and quicker way to understand the nature of jealousy is to marry a pretty and vivacious wife, and wrath in old age can often be demonstrated to a young man who is saucy to a bad-tempered grandfather.

Such elementary knowledge is seemingly too simple for scholars. No historian or psychologist has yet explored "The Effects of Bodily Fatigue on the Course of History." Yet as any soldier knows, after a long and tiring march or a tedious move from one camp to another, all ranks, from colonel to junior private, become peevish, hypersensitive, insubordinate, foul mouthed and unreasonable. Crude bad temper, directly engendered by weariness, is a principal cause of rash judgments, broken marriages, dissipation of cohorts, and the ultimate crashing of empires.

Mild hunger also is as potent a cause of irrational behavior. Menenius knew this well from past experiences with Coriolanus; he would wait till after dinner before venturing into his presence to plead for Rome. Previous missions, he guessed, had failed because

He was not taken well, he had not din'd.
The veins unfill'd, our blood is cold, and then
We pout upon the morning, are unapt
To give or to forgive; but when we have stuff'd
The pipes, and these conveyances of our blood
With wine and feeding we have suppler souls
Than in our priest-like fasts.

Senior officers, especially those whose livers have long been exposed to hot skies, are apt also to pout upon the morning. In 1918 I served as staff captain to a brigadier who was so bad tempered before his lunch that I could communicate with him only by written notes so worded that the required answer was limited to yes or no. When his veins were filled, he was quite charming, sparkling with anecdotes of triumph in field and bed.

Another instance. Ernest Hemingway wrote a short story called "The Short Happy Life of Francis Macomber," wherein the husband, confronting an angry wounded buffalo, is shot—deliberately or accidentally—by his wife. Critics have held lengthy inquest over the body and returned different verdicts: murder or manslaughter. Had any one of them ever fired a 6.5 Mannlicher he would have learned that it kicks like a peevish camel. As he rubbed his bruised and swollen cheek, he would have realized that with such a weapon no woman, whatever her intent, let alone one flustered by so sudden a crisis, could have accurately planted an intentional bullet either in husband or buffalo. This behavior of heavy rifles was doubtless not unknown to Hemingway.

The worst of our modern illusions of the theater is that all experience is explicable in terms of exact science. One most valuable result of the study of literature is that the student is made to realize that there are more things in heaven and in earth—experiences religious, aesthetic, emotional and even physical, on the surface and in the depths—than can be analyzed, controlled or predicted. They come and go at the most unexpected times. We can only hope that given the opportunity they may be ours. We must wait upon the spirit; and the spirit does not submit to laboratory controls. This is the ultimate quarrel between the humanist and those materialists who would deny that anything can exist unless they themselves can comprehend it. In every human mind there are vast areas of insensitive spots; and some of the greatest thinkers, modern or ancient, are misled by failing to realize this limitation.

Since our own experiences are perforce very limited, literary study is the best vicarious substitute. The reader can share whole realms of experience recorded by others more sensitive and perceptive than he and more able to express what they have experienced. He can soar through the gates of Heaven with John on Patmos, suffer with Lear, mock with Donne and Byron, thrill over the dance of the daffodils with Wordsworth, share Caliban's broodings with Browning, lead revolts in the desert with Lawrence, or—if his tastes are that way inclined—he can go drably whoring with James Boswell, and with less risk and expense. At its greatest, recorded experience can be more intense than reality, for the sensitive reader often lives more acutely in his imagination than in daily life. Moreover, when he encounters vital experience in life, he is better equipped to understand it, for he brings his reading to life, which thereby becomes more vital.

The prime purpose of a teacher of literature is to aid his students to grasp the meaning and significance of what they read at all levels. Though it is no part of his duty to tag on a moralizing epilogue, he can hardly avoid at least some indication of his own reactions and sympathies. Nor can he escape the hard fact that for most modern students he has become, however reluctantly, their guide in right thinking and feeling. He must therefore be positive in his own beliefs lest he be a blind mouth feeding wind and rank mist to his hungry sheep.

Literature is great and memorable as the writer expresses clearly what he has to say. By continual contact with clear expression, the student's own thoughts and his power of expressing them increase. Herein lies the justification and the necessity of the disciplined study of the technique of writing in its narrower and wider aspects. That study has also the effect that the more exactly and clearly we try to express our own feelings, ideas and experiences, the more acute and sensitive we become, not only in ourselves but also about what is happening in another's depths. Insensitivity is a major curse of the white races. Too often we hurt by our kindness and best-meaning intentions.

A Japanese Professor of English told me this story. One of his colleagues had an intense, almost passionate, love for the beauties of finely grained wood, with which he had adorned the inside walls of his house. During the occupation of Japan the house was taken over by the military. Eventually they gave it back, and as a gesture of friendliness they first made a very thorough job of repairing all damage. Finally they covered its inside surfaces with two coats of the best glossy enamel paint. The officer in charge still cannot understand why the owner regarded him with such a look of implacable hate.

The art of communication can only be partially taught, for the writer must first have something to communicate. Moreover, he must learn that communication in the depths is conveyed by suggestion, sometimes even by a slight gesture or a glance. The supremest communication often passes in silence, for the greatest writers convey their profoundest meanings by reticence; but reticence is a civilized form of expression, no longer fashionable. So too between teacher and taught, questioning look and answering nod often transmit deeper understanding than the minutest analysis.

The teacher of English thus labors under certain disadvantages compared with his colleagues in other disciplines. By examination and test they can discover what their students have acquired. He cannot so estimate his success or failure. Like the broadcaster, he sends his words into the air; but he receives no fan mail by which to check the responses. Herein lies a danger. A facile teacher with a pleasing personality can easily acquire a kind of popularity very satisfying to his own vanity but evanescent in its results. The thoughts of a less personable teacher ultimately penetrate deeper and last longer; his hearers annex his thoughts as their own, usually without even realizing their origin.

The responsibility of a teacher of English is in truth quite frightening. He cannot be merely a purveyor of information; his own philosophy permeates whatever he offers; his influence is incalculable. Even in the dullest discussion a spark may be dropped which kindles a forest fire in some dry mind. Nor can he shield himself behind the authority of others. The value of what he gives depends upon himself and his personality. In the classroom he stands alone.